AT THE GO
OF TH

A tribute to the men commemorated on the war memorial at

SUTTON - CUM - DUCKMANTON

Michael R. Orme

This book belongs to :

Rowena Hall

Michael R. Orme © 2021

The right of Michael R. Orme to be identified as the Author of this work has been asserted in accordance with the Copyrights, Designs and Patents Act 1988.

British Library Cataloguing In Publication Data
A Record of this Publication is available from the British Library

ISBN 978-1-5272-9921-4

First Published 2021
By

NORMAN TEMPLETON PUBLISHING
ntempletonpub@yahoo.com
CHESTERFIELD

Printed and bound in Great Britain by
www.print2demand.co.uk
Westoning

Fading away like the stars in the morning,
losing their light in the glorious sun.
Thus did they pass from this earth and its toiling,
and were almost forgotten with what they had done.

Who'll sing their anthem? And who'll tell their story?
Did their line hold? Did it scatter and run?
Can they at last be united in glory,
and always remembered for what they had done? *

*These lines are adapted from an original work by John Tams and are used here with his kind permission.

CONTENTS

INTRODUCTION

Every year, a small but dedicated group gathers with great solemnity around the war memorial at Sutton-cum-Duckmanton, by tradition timing their assembly to take place a little over an hour before noon, on what is usually a cold and frequently wet November day. Seen as an essential part of the annual ritual that they are there to re-enact, one amongst their number will almost always recite the words of Lawrence Binyon, inviting a response from all of those present in which they reaffirm a solemn covenant that they will continue to "remember them." The problem with this of course is that nowadays very few of those who choose to brave the autumn elements actually knew any of the men from the parish that fell in even the Second World War. The sun has simply risen and set too many times, and true remembrance has now largely been eroded to the point of extinction by nothing more than the relentless passage of time. Sadly, this is not unique, as we have now reached a point where virtually all of the men and women commemorated on our numerous local memorials have completely slipped out of the realm of living memory. Consequently, we find ourselves in a position where we have merely been left with lists of names, which as the years continue to roll by, are increasingly likely to become meaningless to future generations. The purpose of this work therefore is to ease the passage of those named on the memorial at Sutton-cum-Duckmanton into a new era of commemoration, by allowing at least something of their now largely forgotten stories to be re-told and shared with the wider public.

By bringing together, for the first time, the stories of the men of the parish that are named on its memorial it is hoped that we may be making a contribution towards securing a future for their continued commemoration. Just because we are not in a position to physically remember these men does not mean that we, and indeed subsequent generations, should cease to both accord them our respect and continue to reflect upon the terrible price that was paid by each of them. The losses of each and every one of them should remain important to us, simply because many of the freedoms that we all too frequently take for granted today were at least in part secured for us by their premature deaths. It is, therefore, hoped that by going beyond their names to get a deeper understanding of them as individuals, we can gain a fuller understanding and wider appreciation of their sacrifice. This perhaps becomes particularly important when we consider a widely held belief that, unless we choose to heed the lessons that can be taught by events in our history, we must accept that at some point we are likely to see them repeated. Whilst we may not actually be able to remember, surely, we ought not to forget?

One perhaps neglected aspect of our war memorials is that for many they once held the same significance as real graves. Like the overwhelming majority of these monuments, the one erected in the parish of Sutton-cum-Duckmanton was built to commemorate the dead of the Great War in an era when comparatively few could have afforded to travel and visit the actual final resting places of their fallen kinsmen. Worse still, around half of those who had perished in that conflict would never have their remains identified, and are even now denied the dignity of a known grave. In the inter-war period floral tributes were often laid on our local memorials all the year round to mark birthdays and other family events, and desperately moving stories have survived from our district in later years that tell of flowers being taken from the funerals of the widows or parents of these men to be placed upon them in one final posthumous act of loving remembrance.

Although they now act as a focus for the commemoration for all those who have lost their lives in every conflict since 1914, we should remain aware of this wider significance that our memorials once held for the now long-gone members of those communities that oversaw their creation. Those that had truly known these men in life, and therefore endured the sharpest pain at their loss, are also a part of the story that these monuments tell, and should similarly not be forgotten. This also makes it of vital importance that we should continue to respect and care for the fabric of all of these original memorials everywhere, for collectively they represent the grief that had a profound effect upon our nation as a whole. In that regard, however, the cross at Sutton-cum-Duckmanton seems to be particularly well placed. It is maintained by the local Parish Council whose members not only make up the hard core at those traditional November gatherings, but who have also given their full and enthusiastic cooperation in the production of this volume.

THE HISTORY OF THE MEMORIAL AND NOTES ON THE RESEARCH

Fortunately, we know something about the planning, building and dedication of the memorial at Sutton-cum-Duckmanton, because it was mentioned in the local press in the immediate aftermath of the Great War. The initial steps towards arranging for its erection in the parish seem to have been taken as early as 1919, and the fruition of those preparations, which resulted from the activities of a local planning and fund-raising committee headed by a Mr W. Waplington of Markham House, eventually led to it being officially unveiled amidst scenes of great ceremony on Sunday 24th April 1921. As this local newspaper coverage represents virtually the only source of information that we have concerning the history of the memorial, the article published in The Derbyshire Courier on 30th April 1921 to mark that official unveiling is quoted here in full.

DUCKMANTON'S CROSS

War Memorial Unveiled By Mrs Chas. Markham.

An ornamental stone cross which has been erected by the people of Sutton-cum-Duckmanton as a war memorial at the bottom of Duckmanton Hill was unveiled by Mrs Charles Markham, of Ringwood, on Sunday afternoon.

The service was conducted by the Rev. N. C. Robertson, assisted by Mr E. G. Stanton and Mr W. Timms. The Hymns sung were "O God, our help in ages past," "How bright these glorious spirits shine," and "For all the saints" "Last Post" was sounded by Scouts Hobson and Pailey. At the close of the service many beautiful wreaths and flowers were placed on the steps and round the base of the cross.

Amongst those present were Alderman Eastwood, Mr and Mrs W.

Waplington (Annesley), Mr D. Turner (Duckmanton Lodge), and Dr and Mrs Badcock (Staveley).

The scholars from Duckmanton Sunday School, and the ex-soldiers from Duckmanton and Markham were preceded by Staveley Old Comrades Brass and Reed Band, which also provided the music for the service, and the Boy Scouts Band brought down the Church Sunday School scholars and Primitive Methodists from Arkwright Town.

The memorial was the work of Mr Randall of Hasland.

Sadly, with the exceptions of Alderman Eastwood and Mrs Charles Markham, little is known of the individuals that are named in this report. Be that as it may, the Dr Benjamin and Mrs Bertha Badcock that it connects to the neighbouring district of Staveley are known to have lost their son in the war. Also named Benjamin, he had died of wounds in France at the age of 20 on 9th July 1918 whilst serving as a Lieutenant with the 1st/6th Battalion of the Sherwood Foresters. At the other end of the social scale, however, we are perhaps not taking too much of a liberty to surmise that the Scout referred to simply as *"Hobson"* was likely to have been related to the William Alfred Hobson who will feature later in this work.

The memorial that we see today does differ slightly from its original format, because engraved metal plates were attached to it at a later date to add the names of those local men who had fallen in the Second World War. Unfortunately, these not only covered over the original inscriptions that had been cut directly into the stone plinth that forms the base of the cross, but contain a great number of spelling variations when compared with that original list of names. Indeed, one of the names that we now see listed was so badly transcribed that for many years it was believed that the sacrifice of Charles Banton had gone unrecorded. When that plate was later removed to have his name added however, it was discovered that he had almost certainly been mentioned on the original set of inscriptions as "Bantam, C.". At the same time, it was also noticed that the original inscriptions made no mention of the "Barber, C." whose name does appear on the more modern plate. Though perhaps the most serious, these were far from being the only discrepancies that were found, and a great deal of effort has therefore been expended in discovering the correct form of each name and establishing the true identity of every man that is commemorated here from both of the world wars.

As the original inscriptions on the memorial remain covered by the engraved plates, the details of the original wording which lies beneath them is given here. The front face of the base of the memorial, which faces the Staveley Road, bore the inscription:

IN MEMORY OF THE MEN OF
SUTTON – CUM –
DUCKMANTON
WHO FELL IN THE GREAT WAR
1914 -1918
THEY WERE A WALL UNTO US
BOTH BY NIGHT AND BY DAY

The faces to either side of this both originally bore the names of the Great War casualties, and gave more detail than is contained on the single engraved plate that has superseded them. As these inscriptions are also now covered, they too are transcribed here:

Side 1

J. ATTENBOROUGH
C. BANTAM PTE
W. BARBER SGT
A. BOWLES PTE
W. BOWMAN L. CPL
G. COE SGT
J. CUPITT PTE
J. T. CURREY PTE
A. E. GILHAM PTE
J. W. GLOVER PTE
W. B. GORDON PTE
F. HARRIS PTE
W. HOBSON L. CPL
W. HORNER PTE

Side 2

J. HUDSON PTE
W. E. IND CAPT. M.C.
A. LONGDEN PTE
T. NEWBOLD PTE
W. NEWTON PTE
E. SMITH PTE
A. STONES PTE
R. S. WALLER PTE
A. H. WARDLE PTE
J. E. WARDLE PTE
W. J. WEBBE PTE
E. WILLSON PTE
H. WORTH PTE

It is interesting to note that the parish also has another memorial to its fallen of the Great War, taking the form of a painted wooden tablet that can be found on a wall within St. Mary's Church at Sutton Scarsdale. This memorial is actually useful in several ways, not the least of which being that it confirms the spellings of surnames that were originally cut into the stonework of the cross. Indeed, the only evident variation is that this memorial uses the single "L" version of the surname Willson. In addition, it should be noted that the name "Barber, C." is also absent from this memorial, just as it was from the original stone inscriptions at the foot of the cross.

The discovery of this hitherto unrecorded memorial, however, is not believed to offer any resolution to another mystery that was uncovered during the course of our research. Stemming from a brief report that appeared in the Derbyshire Courier on 12th November 1921, which gives no details concerning either the form it took or the method of its construction, evidence has also been found for the unveiling of *"a Roll of Honour"* at the school in Arkwright Town, on which were listed *"the names of old boys who have served and fallen in the Great War"*. Though this memorial would be of great value to both local historians and genealogists should it ever be rediscovered, it is believed to have been lost many years ago. This could, of course, have contained a substantially different list of names to that which appears on both of the surviving memorials, as many of the men named on them were not old boys of that particular school.

Some reference should also be made in this section concerning the research that has been undertaken to fill the pages that follow. A wide variety of sources have been consulted in the compilation of this work, and whilst many of them are original records that have survived from the periods covered, others have been secondary and are of a more recent date. The most important aspect of all the investigations that have been undertaken has been to use all of these sources as a means to discover a trail of hard evidence to ensure that each of the casualties has been correctly identified. The process for establishing these identifications does, however, vary for each individual, dependent upon the information that can be gleaned from those frequently fragmentary strands of surviving evidence. In order to ensure that all of the investigations have been carried out consistently there has, however, been a guiding methodology that has been strictly adhered to for every name inscribed on the memorial.

The basic principles of this type of research project centre upon

1914 – 1918

J.ATTENBOROUGH	J.GLOVER	W.NEWTON
W.BARBER	W.GORDEN	E.SMITH
C.BARBER	F.HARRIS	A.STONES
H.BOWLES	W.HOBSON	R.WALLER
W.BOWMAN	W.HORNER	A.WARDLE
G.COE	J.HUDSON	T.WARDLE
J.CUPITT	W.IND	W.WEBB
J.CURREY	A.LONGDEN	E.WILSON
A.GILLAM	T.NEWBOLD	H.WORTH
C.BANTON		

The names of the Great War casualties as they currently appear on the memorial.

1939 – 1945

J.K.ALVEY	R.MARPLES
R.W.BRYON	G.PECK
B.CLARKE	J.PENNEY
J.CROOKES	V.PLUM
T.CURRY	K.SIMS
C.G.DANIEL	T.SIMS
R.MADIN	C.WHARTON
W.MOORE	H.WINNARD

R.T.COOPER   E.GLENN   D.W.BLAND

The plate added for the casualties of the Second World War.

finding evidence that establishes a firm series of connections between 3 key criteria. The initial step is simply to make a record of each name as it appears on the memorial. In the case of Sutton-cum-Duckmanton, however, this is not so easy to establish as it may first appear, owing to the numerous spelling errors that are present on the engraved metal plates. It is due to these issues having been identified that the heading for each individual biography uses the name as it currently appears on the memorial, with the full name and corrected spellings shown beneath. These same issues are also responsible for the frequent explanations that have been required to show which of the memorial inscriptions are incorrect, and to outline the supporting evidence behind the conclusions that have been reached in establishing the true identities of the men that they were actually intended to commemorate.

The second criterion that must be fulfilled involves finding a casualty with a name that matches each inscription on the memorial. This also, in most cases, is significantly less simple than the casual observer might imagine. For example, when we try to find a casualty to match the inscription we have for the "Smith, E." who lost his life in the Great War, the records of the Commonwealth War Graves Commission provide us with no fewer than seven hundred and seventy alternatives. A well-known phrase concerning needles and haystacks is indeed one that readily springs into the mind of most memorial researchers at one time or another.

The connection to the third and final criterion is actually the most important of them all. Having recorded a name on the memorial, and identified a casualty who matches that inscription, we must then establish a firm connection between that specific casualty and the parish where he is commemorated. It is only when all three of these stars have been brought into alignment that any tentative identification that we may have been able to establish becomes certain. Unfortunately, however, there are some instances in which making all three of these connections has proved to be impossible, despite the most diligent efforts to find the required supporting evidence.

It is obvious that the engraved metal plates on the memorial originally intended to list the names of the fallen in alphabetical order of surname within each conflict, though an error was made for the casualties of the Second World War where "Moore" was listed before "Marples". The later addition of more names has ruined this effect even further and, therefore, this approach has been changed for the main sections of this volume. Here instead, the men have been placed into the order in which their lives were lost. This has been done to put each fatality into its correct context within the chronology of each of the two wars, allowing us to more readily show how every loss fitted into the way that each of those conflicts developed and evolved. Most other published works on either of these wars also deal with their subjects in strict chronological order, and adopting that same structure here, therefore, also enables this volume to be more easily read alongside those other sources.

To conclude, every effort has been made to ensure that the details given in the following pages are 100% accurate. It does however remain possible that errors may have been made inadvertently, and it is also likely that additional information may come to light in future that may significantly add to our knowledge of these men. The author has no hesitation in unreservedly accepting full responsibility for any such errors or omissions. If anyone has more information about these men, we would welcome those details so that any future editions may be corrected accordingly. We are of course particularly interested in any details concerning the men that we have not yet been able to identify, and in obtaining better quality images of them than those that we have been able to find in the old local newspapers. The vast majority of these were sourced from microfiche copies of the original publications that are held in Chesterfield Public Library.

SECTION ONE

THE GREAT WAR 1914-19

A total of 28 names are currently listed on the memorial that relate to men who lost their lives during the Great War, of which 25 have been identified. As discussed in the section concerning the history of the memorial however, one of the names that we see today was almost certainly placed there in error, as both the original inscriptions in the stonework and the memorial tablet in St. Mary's Church list only 27.

Whilst the individual stories of the men that we have been able to identify occupy many of the pages that follow, it is perhaps possible to get an even greater understanding of the impact that the war had on the wider local community by looking at them as a group. Of course, using such a small sampling size would make it dangerous to try and extrapolate what we can discover concerning these 25 men and expand it into anything that purports to show national trends, but it does perhaps speak reliably about the wider population of the parish over a century ago simply because both they and their families were all closely associated with it. Whilst the following analysis cannot claim to be an all-encompassing and authoritative exploration of all the data that can be extracted and used in this way, it does highlight some areas that may make us want to challenge preconceived opinions about the war and some of the attitudes that we may have today towards the men who fought in it. Certainly, one thing that we should also consider is that, if we do the inverse, and take one national statistic and apply it to the parish, we are using the data compiled concerning just 27 men whilst ignoring what may have been over 240 others from Sutton-cum-Duckmanton who were fortunate enough to have served, fought, and returned.

In common with many of the villages in that local area during the early years of the 20th Century, the parish of Sutton-cum-Duckmanton was experiencing something of a boom. That is not to say that these were happy times for all, because those early years after the death of Queen Victoria bore witness to increasing levels of unrest. For the working classes there were low wages and the spectre of unemployment in a system of social care that still had the Workhouse at its heart. In addition, there was increasing dissatisfaction at the lack of a universal franchise, which left a large proportion of the population without any ability to have a say in how their lives were governed. The industrial boom being experienced in North East Derbyshire during this era, however, meant that there was also opportunity, growth, and at least some prosperity. The village of Arkwright Town, which was the main population centre of the parish at that time, was indeed an example of what was good. The relatively recently built rows of housing there were of better quality than many of those to be found in other districts, and were doubtless a key factor that helped to draw labour into the area to seek work in the expanding mining industry. We can see something of this in the backgrounds of the men named on the memorial, because many of them did not have their origins in the locality. Only 44% of these men actually had their births registered in the Chesterfield district, with others coming from as far afield as the counties of Cambridgeshire, Gloucestershire, Northamptonshire, Shropshire, and Wiltshire.

With reference having been made to the dominance of the Mining Industry in the area at that time, we need only look at the men named on the memorial to find the evidence of how important a part it played in the lives of the local community. At least 84% of these men were employed in that industry before they engaged for military service, and had held a variety of jobs from surface workers and Pony Drivers to Hewers at the coal face. Though it has proved to be impossible to identify all of the collieries where each individual man worked, evidence does exist to show that the vast majority of them were employed at either one of the two Markham pits or the newer Bonds Main Colliery near Temple Normanton. The fact that only one of these men could be described as coming from the professional middle classes also speaks volumes about the parish being a decidedly working-class area. It should, however, be noted that even he began the war as a Corporal, and by talent alone had risen to become an acting Brigade Major before his life was taken.

Perhaps the next important thing to consider would be to try and find some clues concerning the still controversial issue regarding what had motivated these men to enlist. The casualties on the memorial can actually give us some small insight into this, and when we examine them more closely, have a remarkable story to tell. It would probably be fair to say that, despite her Empire, militarism had never had a great following in Britain. This is supported by the fact that only 12% of these men had any connection with the fighting services before war had been declared, and that even their experience could not be described as having been extensive. Only one had already been serving as a soldier of the Regular Army, another was a part-time Reservist, and the third a member of the part-time Territorial Force. Of the remainder, a staggering 80% had freely volunteered *after* war had been declared when the potential danger of taking that step should have been apparent. In fact, only one man identified from the memorial was conscripted, whilst one other had gone into the army via the halfway-house route of the Group Scheme that, in 1915, had been introduced as an alternative to full-blown conscription.

One interesting and perhaps unexpected statistic related to their enlistments demonstrates that over 50% of the 25 identified casualties were married men with children. Whilst the cynic may argue that this tells us much about the state of those marriages, this extremely high proportion can surely not be explained away so glibly. The terrible cost associated with their involvement was not only restricted to 13 of their wives becoming widows, but compounded by the additional suffering of the 28 children who became fatherless. Another widely circulated "fact" about the Great War, for which there is absolutely no evidence on the memorial at Sutton-cum-Duckmanton, is that the army had relied heavily upon gullible under-aged youngsters to fill its ranks. Whilst there is obviously ample evidence to show that this did happen elsewhere, not one single man that has been identified on the parish memorial was recruited under-age. Whilst their average age at death was around 28 years, the eldest amongst them was actually 41 and the youngest 22. The premature loss of every single one of those lives is of course deeply tragic, but perhaps the opinions of our generation should also be tempered by the fact that many of those who did enlist had already been exposed to the very real dangers of working underground from the age of 14 which, in this area and in that era, was not only usual but expected.

All of the above actually begins to point towards these men on the memorial having largely volunteered for reasons of patriotism. Made aware that Britain needed to expand her army by the widely respected Lord Kitchener, they saw the danger of inactivity and took a step forward. Probably the best example we have of this is to be found in the three men (representing 12% of the identified casualties) who are known to initially have been rejected by the army, but who steadfastly refused to accept that decision and were successfully enlisted when they presented themselves on subsequent occasions. This should surely make these men and their sacrifice much more worthy of our continued respect and commemoration, because without those huge numbers of determined and willing volunteers coming forward in the early days of the conflict there can be little doubt that Germany and her allies would have been victorious.

We should of course also be mindful that, when these men did enlist, they almost certainly had no concept of what this war would be like, how long it would last, and how many lives it would claim. Any who had been able to forecast those things would have indeed found themselves in a very small minority at a time when the widely held view was that it would all be over by Christmas 1914. It should also be remembered that the Boer War would have been seen as one of Britain's most serious military challenges prior to 1914, and that in this entire campaign our local regiment had seen fewer than 40 of its men killed in action. There was simply no precedent for the Great War, and none could have had any clue that this same regiment would see over 11,400 of its men lose their lives as a result of Britain becoming engaged in it.

When it came to their enlistment preferences, it is interesting to note the numbers that chose to join the local Sherwood Foresters (Notts & Derby) Regiment. Over 50% of the identified casualties on the memorial either died with them or had originally attested for service with them before later being transferred to other units. Men from the parish actually lost their lives whilst serving with no fewer than 8 different battalions of this regiment. Whilst this reflects what we find on most of the other memorials in the district, it stands in stark contrast with the wide variety of different units that we find amongst the local casualties that resulted from the Second World War. Though the high proportion of volunteers that chose to serve in the local regiment during the Great War is perhaps unsurprising, some of the other units represented are perhaps more difficult to understand. The fact that three of these local lads chose to join Scottish regiments may at first seem inexplicable, but they were not unique, and evidence of this is also found on other local memorials. In some cases, those who had enlisted underage chose this option to make it harder for their families to trace them, in others there may have been older family associations with these regiments, or it may simply have been that these units were especially admired because of their history, traditions or uniforms.

There are perhaps some surprises concerning the places where the casualties from the village fought and died. We have examples of men who lost their lives on the now often forgotten battlefields of Mesopotamia (modern day Iraq) and Italy. We have another who, though not killed there, could be viewed as having indirectly lost his life because of wounds that he had received at Gallipoli. Rather less surprisingly over 50% of them were killed in France, whilst death both sought and found a further 32% of them in Belgium. With the sites of their graves and places of official commemoration scattered far and wide it is perhaps easy to overlook the two men who were buried in the churchyard at Duckmanton, despite the fact that their lives were lost whilst wearing the King's uniform and that their sacrifice is therefore equally deserving of our commemoration and respect.

Men from the parish fell in every year of the war, though only one life was lost in 1914. The identified casualties on the memorial actually show how the mortality grew year on year before falling back in the final year of the conflict. Four were lost in 1915, six in 1916, eight in 1917, and six in the final year to the Armistice. By using the records of the Commonwealth War Graves Commission we can actually see how this compares with the losses that were incurred nationally. In order to do this their figures for deaths occurring annually have been filtered to use only the totals for British casualties that were serving in the army, because all of the men on the memorial that we have been able to identify (with the exception of Horner who was fighting with the Australians) fall into those categories. The results show a startling similarity in terms of how well the losses in the parish mirrored those that were experienced countrywide. In the following analysis the % losses of the parish are followed by the national % figures for each year.

1914	4.0%	and	3.8%
1915	16.0%	and	16.1%
1916	24.0%	and	24.2%
1917	32.0%	and	29.0%
1918	24.0%	and	26.8%

When it comes to their final resting places, the dead of the parish actually fared better than most. Nationally, approximately 50% of the casualties of the Great War have no known graves and therefore receive their official commemorations on the many memorials to the missing that are under the control of the Commonwealth War Graves Commission. By contrast, only 40% of the dead named at Sutton-cum-Duckmanton are honoured in this way, with the 60% majority having been interred at known locations in plots which are marked by individual headstones that bear their names. It should, however, be noted that this does not necessarily mean that those named on the official memorials to the missing did not receive a proper burial, as those rites were also accorded to any sets of remains that were recovered but which could not be identified. Their graves are to be found scattered across many cemeteries, with headstones bearing the simple inscription "known unto God" that was specifically selected for this purpose by Rudyard Kipling. Sadly, it does, however, remain true that many of the fallen were simply never found. Even a century later the remains of the dead are still being discovered every year on the old battlefields of the Great War, and they are still being respectfully interred at the beautifully maintained cemeteries of the Commonwealth War Graves Commission.

It is interesting to note, and seldom realised that, where newly discovered sets of remains can be identified, the names of those men are removed from the memorials to the missing after they have been interred. This is not only fitting because they are then counted amongst those who have known graves, but also satisfies the strict ethos of the Commission which dictates that each casualty should receive only one commemoration, thereby ensuring that, because they all made the same sacrifice, they are all treated equally in death. The same, however, can not be said of the legacy that has been left to us in the form of our beautiful and divers local memorials. As they were all brought into being independently of each other, it is not uncommon to find that commemorations of the same individuals are frequently repeated on several of them.

THE FALLEN
OF
THE GREAT WAR
1914 - 1919

Albert Edward Gilham	21st December 1914
Wilfred Newton	16th June 1915
Thomas Newbold	9th August 1915
John William Hudson	26th September 1915
William Beacham Gordon	21st October 1915
Allison Stones	17th March 1916
Richard Sturley Waller	22nd April 1916
Arthur William Bowles	1st July 1916
John Edward Wardle	4th July 1916
Charles Percival Banton	9th August 1916
William Joseph Warren Webb	24th September 1916
George E. Coe	11th April 1917
Walter Ernest Horner	16th April 1917
William Barber	14th May 1917
William Ernest Ind	7th June 1917
John Cupit	27th June 1917
William Bowman	30th July 1917
Herbert Worth	3rd October 1917
Albert Henry Wardle	13th October 1917
Frederick Alfred Harris	14th July 1918
Ernest Smith	14th July 1918
John William Glover	15th October 1918
Albert Longden	27th October 1918
William Alfred Hobson	13th November 1918
John Thomas Currey	30th December 1918
J. Attenborough	Unidentified
C. Barber	Unidentified
E. Wilson (or Willson)	Unidentified

BIOGRAPHIES OF THOSE WHO FELL IN THE GREAT WAR

GILLAM, A.

ALBERT EDWARD GILHAM

Albert did not have a long-standing connection with Sutton – Cum – Duckmanton, and was born towards the end of 1887 at Harston in Cambridgeshire where his father William was a General Labourer. As late as the 1911 Census, Albert was working as a Waggoner on a farm and lodging at a house on Market Street in Woodhouse, Sheffield. It is, however, likely that he moved into Derbyshire shortly afterwards, as he is known to have taken up employment in the local mining industry.

We can perhaps be more certain that he probably only met local girl Mabel May Saunders after he had come into the parish. She had been born at Markham in 1893, and is known to have still been living at Sutton-cum-Duckmanton in 1911. The couple were married in 1913 and went on to have their first and only child, also named Albert Edward, later in that same year.

Fortunately, a few fragments of his army paperwork survive which allow us to establish that Albert Edward Gilham was living at 79, Scarsdale Road, Carr Vale with his wife and child when war was declared. When pieced together, these various documents tell us a remarkable story about how determined Albert had been to answer the call of his country.

His surviving pension records show that he enlisted into the Royal Artillery at Chesterfield on 1st September 1914, less than a month after war had been declared. Giving his occupation as *"Miner*

Engineer", he also declared that he had previously served for 2 years with the Royal Engineers. Unfortunately, however, Albert was dismissed from the Artillery on 19th October. The phrase *"Physically unfit for war service"* is crossed out on his record, and replaced with the words *"not likely etc"*, which is an abbreviation of the standard phrase *"Not likely to become an efficient soldier."* It must have been a devastating blow to him at the time, but we shall see that he was determined not to be beaten by it.

None of Albert's detailed records survive for his time with the Northamptonshire Regiment, but the issue of his 16180 service number can be dated to on or shortly after the 27th October 1914. We also know that he enlisted with them in Nottingham, perhaps out of concern that he might have been recognised if he had returned to see the recruiting staff in Chesterfield. That this is the same Albert Gilham can, however, be proven by using other surviving records for this soldier of the Northamptonshire Regiment, which not only confirm that he had been born in Harston but also show that his widow was named *"Mabel M."*

We also know that Albert spent very little time in training, because he landed in France as part of a reinforcement draft for the 1st Battalion of the regiment on 12th November 1914. They had been in France as part of the 1st Division of the British Expeditionary Force since 13th August and had already endured much bitter fighting, having been involved in the Battles of Mons, The Marne and The Aisne. At the time that Albert landed they were just being pulled out of the line after having also had a role in what would later become known as the First Battle of Ypres. That they were in sore need of reinforcements can be judged from their war diary entry for 15th November which states that, as they headed out of Belgium for a period of reconstruction at Strazeele in France, their total strength had been reduced to less than 30% of what it had been when they landed. All that remained of that original battalion amounted to just 2 officers and 300 enlisted men.

Albert lost his life on 21st December 1914 at the age of 27, and the battalion war diary informs us that his unit had not moved back into the line (in the vicinity of Le Touret), until that same day. Upon their arrival, they immediately took part in a night attack which was launched at 19:00 hrs, tasked with recovering trenches that had previously been lost to the Germans. It is therefore likely that

Albert was killed during the early stages of that operation. Whilst the cause of his death was officially recorded as "Died of wounds" it is more likely that he was actually killed outright, as this would more readily explain why he has no known grave. Just like the other men from his unit who were recorded as having been "Killed in Action" that day, he therefore receives his official commemoration on the memorial to the missing at Le Touret.

So far as is known Albert was the first man included on the parish memorial to have fallen in the war. He is however currently commemorated incorrectly on two of the local memorials by being named as "Gillam" at Duckmanton and "Gilham, A. L." on the memorial cross that stands in Bolsover Market Place. Both the original recording of his name on the stonework of the memorial at Sutton-cum-Duckmanton and the plaque inside St. Mary's church, however, list his name correctly as "Gilham, A. E."

NEWTON, W.

WILFRED NEWTON

In 1921, HMSO published a colossal work entitled "Soldiers Died in The Great War 1914-19". Despite only covering the enlisted men of the army that had perished during the conflict, and giving the barest details about each of them using information extracted from their service records, it ran to a staggering 80 volumes. It was, however, this source which first identified Pte. 15884, Wilfred Newton of the Grenadier Guards as having been born at Duckmanton. Additional information held by the Commonwealth War Graves Commission tells us that he was the *"Son of Thomas and Elizabeth Newton, of 72, Station Rd., New Brimington, Chesterfield, Derbyshire."* It seems highly likely, however, that the family had only moved to that address after the war had ended, as he is only remembered at Duckmanton and receives no mention on either of the two surviving memorials in Brimington.

His extensive obituary in the Derbyshire Times clearly states that when the news of his death reached his mother, she was living at 31, Arkwright Town. This therefore both connects him with the parish and confirms his identification as the man named on the memorial. Further confirmation is found in the 1911 census which also shows the family at that same Arkwright Town address, and describes the then 17-year-old Wilfred as being employed as a *"Colliery Pony Driver Below {Ground}."* His obituary adds the further detail that he had in fact been working at Markham No 1 Colliery prior to his enlistment.

One point of interest is that Wilfred's father is named on the 1911 census as George and, as he both filled out and signed the return documents, the records of the Commonwealth War Graves

Commission would initially seem to be in error by naming him as Thomas. This discrepancy is perhaps resolved by consulting the records for his marriage which, in addition to informing us that the maiden name of his wife Elizabeth had been Hadley, gives his full name as George Thomas Newton. The birth of Wilfred seems to have been recorded in the Chesterfield district during the March ¼ of 1893 and, though this document therefore slightly contradicts the age of 21 that we have already been given for him at death, it additionally shows that he may have had Edgar as a 2nd Christian name.

We know from "Soldiers Died...." that Wilfred enlisted into the Grenadier Guards at Chesterfield, and his obituary tells us that this occurred in May of 1912. Using the evidence provided by his 15884 service number however, we can more accurately determine that this event is most likely to have occurred between the 15th-22nd of that month. His obituary also tells us a little more about his early service, by stating that he was first sent to Aldershot before later being stationed at Wellington Barracks in Westminster. Then, as now, this regiment was considered to be an elite, having a proud history that stretched back into the middle of the 17th Century. Known as the 1st Regiment of Foot Guards from 1665, they had actually received their additional "Grenadier" title in recognition of their valiant service at the Battle of Waterloo in 1815.

Whilst the records of the Commonwealth War Graves Commission tell us that Wilfred was serving with the 1st Battalion of the regiment when his life was lost, both his Medal Index Card and the Roll for the 1914 Star confirm that he did not arrive in France until 8th November 1914. He could not, therefore, have been an original member of that battalion, which had landed at Zeebrugge on the 7th October as a unit of the 20th Brigade within the 7th Division. The history of the regiment records that two parties of reinforcements joined the battalion at Meteren on the 10th and 11th November respectively, and Wilfred would therefore almost certainly have been amongst one of those drafts. Further clues to his service can be found in his obituary which states that *"he was in the thick of the fighting, and emerged unscathed until March last {1915}, when he received wounds in the arm {which} rendered him hors de combat for nearly three months."* The injury referred to here was almost certainly sustained whilst the battalion was heavily involved in the Battle of Neuve Chapelle, an engagement where the total number of casualties that they sustained amongst all ranks was recorded at 341, or approximately 30% of their total establishment.

Being able to calculate that he probably returned to active service with the battalion in June 1915, he could only have spent a very short time with them before being killed in action on the 16th of that month. Turning again to the battalion history, the timing of Wilfred's death coincides with their involvement in a minor attack launched from an area of the line that lay in front of the French settlements of Festubert and Givenchy. They suffered 63 casualties amongst their enlisted men here, many of which were caused by delays due to waiting for other units on their flanks to catch up. They also, however, encountered further difficulties when crossing German barbed wire entanglements that the supporting British artillery had been unable to cut. A letter from one of his NCO's describing how he had died was published as part of his obituary, stating that:

"I write today to inform you of the death of our dear comrade, Wilfe Newton, your loving son who fell in action on Wednesday 16th June, from wounds received. He passed quietly away within half an hour of being hit after we had done all in our power to relieve his pain. Your son was a good soldier and as a comrade I shall miss him very much."

Sadly, despite adding that *"His last resting place is marked with a cross, with number, name and date inscribed, not many yards from where he fell."*, Wilfred's grave later became lost. He therefore receives his official commemoration on the Le Touret Memorial to the missing which lies in the Pas-de-Calais region of Northern France.

NEWBOLD, T.

THOMAS NEWBOLD

Despite his entry in "Soldiers Died...." stating that Thomas had been born in Derby, this happy event had actually occurred in the Chesterfield district, and almost certainly took place at Beeley during 1889. He was the son of Coal Miner John Newbold and his wife Ann (Brown), and the census for 1891 shows us that the family were then living on Henry Street in Whittington. It is also interesting to note that the Commonwealth War Graves Commission incorrectly name his mother as "Hannah", a statement not only contradicted by her marriage registration and 3 census returns, but also by Thomas's surviving service record.

By 1901 the family had moved to Brimington Common, and a decade after that were living at Lower Alley in Calow. By this date Thomas was employed in the local mining industry as a Hewer at Bonds Main Colliery. His connection with the military had, however, commenced at some time prior, when he had enlisted into the 3rd (Special Reserve) Battalion of the Sherwood Foresters on a 6 year engagement. We know that this event took place at Chesterfield on 1st September 1909, and that his 3170 service number would have been issued at that time.

An enlistment into the Special Reserve battalion of a regiment was essentially a part-time commitment, though it was still associated with the structure of the full-time Regular Army. By contrast, Britain's other part-time soldiers of the Territorial Force, though having close associations with the regiments of the Regular army, were actually members of a completely different and separately run organisation. Thomas would have received full-time training at the regimental depot in Derby for a period of several months, for which he would have received the same payment as a full-time regular. After that, he would have returned back to civilian life and been paid a retainer with the obligation to attend the Depot for further periods of training every year. Unlike the men of the Territorial Force, Thomas was automatically obliged to serve overseas in the event that any national crisis resulted in a general mobilisation.

There was however, another dramatic change in his fortunes before war was declared in August 1914, because he had met a local girl named Florence Gertrude Fletcher and married her during the early months of 1912. Thomas's service papers also make it clear that the couple had gone on to have a son named Willie Newbold who was destined to be their only child.

Other information contained in Thomas's service papers provide us with the evidence of his direct connection with the parish of Sutton-cum-Duckmanton, by confirming that at some point after the 1911 census had been conducted, his parents had moved to take up residence at 57, Arkwright Town. Interestingly, these papers also allow us a glimpse of the man himself, by informing us that he had brown eyes and dark brown hair. They additionally not only confirm that his faith was Church of England, but even tell us that he was 5' 6 ½" tall, weighed 138 lbs and had a 1" scar on his left elbow!

When war was declared, the Special Reserve was mobilised and Thomas was called to join the regiment, though throughout the conflict the 3rd Battalion that had trained him never served overseas as a formed body. It was instead their prime function to provide replacements and reinforcements for the Regular 1st and 2nd battalions of the regiment. He therefore only served with the 3rd Battalion from 1st September to the 10th of November 1914, and landed in France as a very early reinforcement for the 2nd Battalion on the following day. This unit was the direct descendant of the old 95th (Derbyshire) Regiment of Foot which had first been raised in 1823. As they had conveniently been on home service in Sheffield at the beginning of the war, they had landed in France (as part of 18th Brigade in the 6th Division) just one month before Thomas joined them. They were actually the first battalion of the Sherwood Foresters to land in France during the Great War, because their comrades in the 1st Battalion were at that time serving in India. In the brief time that the 2nd Battalion had been on active service before Thomas joined them, they had, however, already seen severe fighting on both the Aisne heights and around Armentiers.

The published history of the 1st and 2nd Battalions of the Sherwood Foresters in the Great War informs us that on 9th August 1915 (the date on which, at the age of 25, Thomas was killed), the 2nd Battalion had played a major role in an attack that had taken place at Hooge in the Ypres sector. The total strength of the unit at the outset was recorded as being 989 men of all ranks, of which just over 11.5% were either killed, or died of wounds. Interestingly, it also records that the men of "A" Company (in which Thomas is known to have served), were amongst the first British troops to go into action equipped with a trial batch of steel helmets.

After initially being declared as "missing" on 9th September, the news of his death was not conveyed to his widow until 28th, when she received a letter from his friend, 14025 Private Robert Edward Brewin. In it he informed her that *"I am very sorry to tell you that your husband has been killed. He was killed in the charge at Hooge, being blown up in the air with a shell, and we saw nothing more of him. I can tell you that he went to the fight with a brave heart, and he died a soldier's death."* Sadly, Private Brewin, who was from Wigston in Leicestershire, was also destined not to survive the war and lost his life on 9th February 1917.

Thomas's body was never identified, and he therefore receives his official commemoration on the Menin Gate Memorial at Ypres. His name may be found there amongst those of 54,606 others who have no known graves and that perished on that sector of the front before 16th August 1917. His only commemorations in the Chesterfield district are on the memorials at Sutton-cum-Duckmanton and Sutton Scarsdale.

HUDSON, J.

JAMES WILLIAM HUDSON

 The birth of James Hudson was recorded in the Doncaster registration district during the September quarter of 1891, though evidence contained in the 1911 census is more specific about this event, showing that it had actually taken place in the parish of Denaby. Both he and his family had, however, relocated to the parish of Sutton-cum-Duckmanton by 1900, where they had taken up residence at 23, Arkwright Town.

Fortunately, we have a surviving service record for James which informs us that he had enlisted in Chesterfield on 25th January 1915 at the age of 23 years and 6 months. These same papers also confirm that his home address had remained unchanged and that he had previously been employed as a Miner. In addition, they also supply us with the information that his mother's maiden name had been Mary Brewster.

This service record also helps us to gain some insight into his early training by informing us that, issued with the service number 17001, he had originally enlisted into the 9th (Service) Battalion of the Royal Scots Fusiliers. Embodied for wartime service, this unit had initially been raised at Gourock in October 1914 and were initially envisaged as being a part of Lord Kitchener's 4th "New Army". In April 1915 however, they were converted into a "reserve" battalion and moved to Paisley. Their function now became one of a depot and training unit responsible for providing replacements and reinforcements for the other battalions of the regiment that were already on active service overseas.

The "Service" battalions that began to be raised shortly after the outbreak of war were the means by which the Regular British Army sought to expand to meet the challenges of fighting against the vast continental armies that had been a product of conscription. Up until the introduction of the Military Service Act in 1916, these battalions, just like their counterparts in the Regular peace-time standing army, were composed entirely of volunteers. The early years of the Great War, in a record that is never likely to be surpassed, actually saw Britain raise the largest volunteer-based fighting force in her entire history. The introduction of these new "Service" battalions also allowed their recruits to enlist on new "Short Service" terms, for a period of "3 years or the duration of the war", and it was actually this new style of contract which James had signed. When he first arrived in France he was still technically a member of the 9th Battalion, but was rapidly reassigned to join the 7th on the 19th August 1915, the day after he landed.

The 7th Battalion (a unit of the 45th Brigade in the 15th (Scottish) Division) had first landed in France as recently as 9th July, making James a very early reinforcement. They had, however, already served in the trenches and suffered casualties before he arrived. A note in the War Diary entry for 21st August mentions the arrival of a draft of 1 Sergeant and 27 men from the 9th Battalion, and James is likely to have been amongst this party when they joined their new unit at Mazingarbe, about 17 miles to the South West of Lille in Northern France.

Sadly, James was destined to fall, at the age of 25, on 26th September 1915, just 36 days after joining this battalion. Interestingly, "Soldiers Died...." gives his cause of death as "Died", which is a coded way of saying that his loss was not directly connected with any activity of the enemy. In this instance however, we can be certain that this was not the case, as the greater detail contained in his service record clearly shows that he was initially listed as "missing in action". We should also note that he has no known grave, and that the date of his death actually coincided with the second day of the Battle of Loos.

Their War Diary records that the 7th Battalion left Grenay at 04:00 hrs on 25th September to take up positions formerly held by the 10th Gordon Highlanders. James and his comrades would, however, only remain there until 09:00 hrs, the time that had been appointed for them to rise up and begin their advance on Loos. For the first hour, they gained ground and suffered only light casualties, but

German resistance stiffened as they reached the vicinity of a feature on the battlefield known as Hill 70. An enemy counter-attack during the night was successfully repulsed, and a further unsuccessful attack by the men of the 7th Battalion was launched at 09:00 hrs on the following day which continued until 17:00 hrs.

The toll on the 7th Battalion was a heavy one, and the casualty figures given for those 2 days in their War Diary show that over 40% of them were either killed, wounded or declared as missing. Evidence from the obituary printed for his friend William Gordon actually confirms that James was originally listed as falling into both of those last two categories and, as his body was never identified, he subsequently received his official commemoration on the Loos Memorial to the missing. This memorial also records the names of over 20,000 others who shared a similar fate on that sector of the front during the Great War.

GORDEN, W.

WILLIAM BEACHAM GORDON

 William Beacham Gordon was the son of Arthur Beacham Gordon and Amelia Ann (Spolding), and had his birth recorded in the Chesterfield registration district during the December quarter of 1892. The use of "Beacham" as a middle name seems to have been something of a tradition within the Gordon family, which also had another branch that was living in Arkwright when the 1911 Census was conducted. Their "Head of household" was William's uncle, Edwin Beacham Gordon, who confusingly also had a son named William Beacham Gordon. He, however, could be excluded from our enquiries because he was actually only 3 years old when that census had been conducted.

The household of Arthur Beecham Gordon was not living too far distant from that of Edwin, with their home in 1911 documented as having been on Works Row, Calow, Chesterfield. This same census informs us that both father and son were then involved in the local mining industry, with William declaring his occupation to have been *"Pony Driver."* It is interesting to note that the plates added to the memorial at Sutton-cum-Duckmanton use a spelling of his surname that is undoubtedly incorrect, as every other record that has been discovered for both William and all the members of his family consistently show that it ended with "ON" rather than "EN".

One of the many documents consulted to confirm this man's identity was the Army Register of Soldiers Effects, which states that William's gratuity was paid to his mother "Amelia A." The payment of his gratuity to her, however, is actually another strange anomaly, because his obituary tells us that William had in fact married a Miss Jane Willis, and from the registration data we find that their wedding had been recorded in the Chesterfield district during the June ¼ of 1914. Whilst the same obituary also informs us that the couple had gone on to have a child together, no matching entry has been found for that event amongst the registration data. There is, however, an entry for a birth in the Chesterfield district during 1915 of a John B. Willis, making it tempting for us to speculate that the "B." may indicate that Beacham had once again found favour as a middle name.

His obituary also furnishes us with a fascinating military themed anecdote, informing us that William had been the grandson of the late Mr W. Gordon. The family were obviously no strangers to either military service or the horrors of war, as we are told that he had not only fought in the Indian Mutiny of 1857, but had lost a leg as a result of wounds that he had received during that campaign.

Our research also revealed several interesting facts concerning William's own involvement with the military. The first of these should perhaps be that his 17002 service number is consecutive with that of James William Hudson (17001) who also enlisted into the Royal Scots Fusiliers and, as we have already seen, is also commemorated on the parish memorial. On consulting his obituary, it is therefore hardly surprising to discover confirmation that the two men had been friends. It is perhaps interesting to speculate on what may have influenced their decision to join a Scottish regiment but, as they both enlisted into the same unit, in the same place, on the same day, and had then both landed in France together on the 18th August 1915, it can be assumed that the details concerning William's early service would have closely mirrored those that we have already outlined for Hudson. We are additionally told in William's obituary that he also had 3 cousins who were serving with the Colours in France, whilst a 4th was in Serbia. It could perhaps therefore have been the case that they had all enlisted together.

William, like Hudson, doubtless also served with the 7th Battalion of the regiment during the Battle of Loos, which was fought over the perhaps familiar looking territory of a French coal mining district. Opening on the 25th September, this battle consisted of a series of engagements which ran through to the 8th October. As such it was the largest British attack of 1915, and represented the first major trial of the "Service" battalions of Lord Kitchener's

"New Army". Ultimately the Battle of Loos achieved very little, though for a brief period on its first day it came very close to making the decisive breakthrough of the German defences that had been its objective.

William managed to survive that battle, but would lose his life shortly afterwards on 21st October 1915. The circumstances of his death were, however, very different to those of Hudson as, rather than being engaged in the maelstrom of an attack, he was simply on duty as part of the day-to-day routine of holding the reserve trenches close to the front line. On this occasion, "Soldiers Died…" describes him as being killed in action and, though it does not mention him by name, the entry for that day in the Battalion War Diary fully corroborates this. It reports that the battalion was in trenches to the south of Hulluch when, at 15:00 hrs, the men of "A" Company were subjected to a heavy artillery barrage. It then goes on to state that their *"A Company lost 4 killed and 5 wounded."* As they reported no other casualties on that date, we can safely assume that William would have been one of them.

His obituary quotes from the contents of an extensive and detailed letter that was written to his widow by a Sergeant Holmes in which he says:

"It is with the greatest regret that I write you a letter of this description. It will be a relief for you to know that your dear husband met his death like a true British soldier. He was fearless and brave – qualities that make a soldier – and I am sure all the platoon will feel his loss. As one of the lads said when he heard about it, "what a pity, he was one of the best." We were in the support trenches and after dinner I had a walk along to see that everything was all right. Your husband was reading the daily paper, and I stopped and chatted with him, and we ventilated our views on the war. He had a pipe of tobacco with me as I had received a parcel the day before. He said he was expecting one. Well, I left him, being called away. I had not been gone 20 minutes when one of the lads came running to me saying that a shell had burst in the trench. Naturally, I ran to the spot, and to my sorrow I found 3 killed and 1 wounded. Knowing your husband I identified him at first glance. The three heroes were buried side by side together the same night. I might say he was not struck with the shell, but the concussion caused his death – what we call "Shell-

Shock." Death was instantaneous, and he suffered no pain. I now take the opportunity of expressing my sympathy on behalf of the lads who were in his platoon. I hope this letter will be a comfort to you, whilst you are undergoing your great and trying ordeal.

In addition to William being remembered with Hudson on both of the parish memorials, the two friends are also fittingly commemorated together on the memorial to the missing at Loos.

STONES, A.

ALLISON STONES

The information given for Allison in "Soldiers Died…." both informs us that he had been born in Staveley, and also provides us with his very unusual Christian name. As we move on to consult other sources however, sometimes this first name is seen written with two "L's" and at others with only one. The correct spelling can however be confirmed as "Allison", as he appears under this spelling in the record that was made for the registration of his birth. We also find it written this way on his Medal Index Card, the Medal Rolls, and in the Register of Soldiers Effects. All three of these military sources would have taken this spelling from his official service record, which sadly seems not to have survived.

His entry on the 1911 Census not only corroborates the information already found in "Soldiers Died…." concerning his place of birth, but additionally connects him with the parish of Sutton-cum-Duckmanton by showing that he was then living as a boarder at 28, Arkwright Town. Two other members of the Stones family are also shown as being boarders at this same address, and all three of them were employed in the local mining industry. From his obituary, we know that Allison was actually employed at Bonds Main Colliery. Having such a unique name also allows the registration of his birth to be found quite easily, and shows us that this was recorded in the Chesterfield district during the September ¼ of 1882. We can therefore calculate that he would have been 33 years old when his life was lost.

From his 16960 service number, we can deduce that Allison is most likely to have joined the regiment on a date close to the 11th November 1914, and from "Soldiers Died…." we also know that he enlisted at Hemsworth in Yorkshire. His obituary actually documents that he had previously tried to enlist in Chesterfield on two separate occasions but had been rejected both times.

Though we cannot be certain that he did not receive his basic training with another unit of the York and Lancaster Regiment, it seems highly likely that he may have been a "founder member" of the 9th (Service) Battalion, because he landed on the same date that the whole of that unit began its overseas service. They were a part of Lord Kitchener's 3rd "New Army" and were raised in Pontefract, though they soon moved away from that area and were stationed at a succession of different locations in the UK before being sent to France. On an amusing note, the cap badge of this regiment, which features both an Indian tiger and a Yorkshire rose, was rather irreverently known to its members as the "cat and cabbage".

The 9th Battalion were a part of 70th Brigade which served in the 23rd Division, and after landing at Boulogne on 27th August 1915, they underwent a process of "trench familiarisation" before taking over a section of the front line to the South East of Hazebrouck, in the vicinity of Merris and Vieux-Berquin. From there they moved a little way further to the South East and occupied positions close to Bois-Grenier, which lies a short distance to the South East of Armentieres.

A few days prior to Allison's death, before they moved out to occupy the trenches, the battalion had been in billets at Fleurbaix. Though this was seen as a quiet sector at that time, there was still intermittent activity by the artillery of both sides, and the Battalion War Diary entry for the date of his death, 17th March 1916, states that the 8" howitzers of the Royal Garrison Artillery had fired eleven shells into the German positions to their front at 16:00 hrs. Perhaps predicably, the enemy artillery retaliated shortly afterwards, killing one man and wounding 2 others. Though he is not mentioned by name, this diary entry must therefore relate to the death of Allison Stones.

His final resting place, and the site of his official commemoration, is at the Rue-David Military Cemetery at Fleurbaix in northern France. His only commemorations in the Chesterfield district are on the memorials at Sutton-cum-Duckmanton and Sutton Scarsdale.

WALLER, R.

RICHARD STURLEY WALLER

 The birth of Richard Sturley Waller was recorded in the Chesterfield registration district during the December ¼ of 1893, and the 1911 Census not only shows us that he was then living with his parents Benjamin and Elizabeth (Knight) in Shuttlewood, but also confirms the fact that he had been born in Duckmanton. He is shown as being 17 years old when that census was conducted, and was working as a *"Rope Boy"* in the local mining industry. His father was also working in the same industry at that date as a Colliery Deputy.

Further information from his obituary tells us that before the war Richard had been a Sergeant Instructor with the Shuttlewood Company of the Church Lads Brigade, and that he had also held the rank of Lieutenant in the Poolsbrook Company of the Church Boys Brigade. An even firmer connection to the parish of Sutton-cum-Duckmanton is, however, established by this source, which states that his parents were living at an address in Markham Cottages when they received the news of his death.

No surviving service records have been identified for Richard, so we have needed to use other sources to determine something of his time in the military. His entry in "Soldiers Died...." is in conflict with the 1911 Census by giving his place of birth as Staveley, but confirms that he had enlisted in Chesterfield. His obituary states that he volunteered on 25th May 1915, and his Medal Roll entries and Medal Index Card both show that he first served overseas from 2nd October in that same year. These documents also demonstrate that the "qualifying service" for his medals had begun in France with the 7th (Service) Battalion of the Seaforth Highlanders. As this unit had first landed in France during May 1915 as part of the 26th Brigade in the 9th (Scottish) Division, we can therefore be certain that Richard had been a later reinforcement rather than an original member of that battalion. We can also be certain that, at some point, he was re-assigned to the "Regular" 1st Battalion with whom he would be killed on 22nd April 1916. His early training in Britain could either have been provided by the 3rd (Reserve) or 10th (Reserve) Battalions, but sadly no evidence has been found which enables us to narrow that down any further.

One mystery, however, was solved by the contents of an article that appeared in an edition of "The Scotsman" that was published on 17th November 1915. It reported that:

"Early yesterday morning an ambulance train with 98 wounded soldiers from France arrived at the Edinburgh War Hospital at Bangour. The train travelled direct from the South coast to the station in the hospital grounds. Among the party were 3 officers and, of the non commissioned officers and men, about one-third belonged to Scottish regiments."

Included in the accompanying list of names is that of 8599 R. S. Waller of the 7th Battalion Seaforth Highlanders. His obituary not only confirms this connection, but informs us that his evacuation back to Britain had resulted from him suffering a form of illness known as "Trench Foot". This debilitating condition arose owing to prolonged exposure of the lower limbs to cold water, and in the most severe cases actually necessitated amputation. Though known in the army since the days of the Crimean War, its resurgence in the Great War initially took the authorities by surprise, precisely because they had experienced little in the way of prolonged trench warfare since the fall of Sebastopol in 1855. Daily foot inspections carried out by officers, improved pumping and drainage, and better protective clothing in the form of "trench waders" meant that it became much less of an issue in the later years of the war. When Richard contracted this condition his unit had been in the trenches near Hill 60 in the Ypres sector.

Turning our attention to the "Regular" 1st Battalion of the regiment, we know that they had moved to Mesopotamia (modern day Iraq) and landed at Basra in late December 1915. Once again, his obituary makes things a little clearer by informing us that he was drafted to Mesopotamia with the 1st Battalion on 14th January 1916, immediately after he had returned to health. Therefore, this makes him part of a sorely needed reinforcement draft. The 1st Battalion of the Seaforths had actually suffered such a great number of casualties in that theatre of war that, by February of 1916, their remnants had joined forces with those of the 2nd Battalion of the Black Watch to form a composite unit that was styled as the "Highland Battalion."

With Richard's new unit serving as a part of the 19th (Dehra Dun) Brigade, of the 7th (Meerut) Division of the Indian Army, we should perhaps look at something of the background to the fighting in what to many has now become a forgotten front of the Great War. Having for centuries been part of the old Ottoman Empire, the rulers of Mesopotamia had only begun to come under the influence of the Kaiser's Germany in the years that led up to the conflict. Despite already being bound to Germany by treaty prior to the time that war was declared, the Ottoman Turks did not take an active role in the conflict until they carried out a raid on the Russian ports of the Black Sea during October 1914. In retaliation, Russia swiftly declared war on these new enemies, triggering a response from the other Allied nations which saw both Britain and France follow suit during November.

British attempts to gain a rapid end to the war in this theatre by seizing the capital Baghdad had not only failed during 1915, but resulted in their attacking force being forced to retreat to Kut-Al-Amara, where they became cut off from their supply lines and besieged. The relief of that force, therefore, became a prime objective, and though various attempts were made to lift the siege, none of them would ever prove to be successful. Richard was actually killed in action at the Battle of Sannaiyat on 22nd April 1916, which represented the final attempt made to relieve the beleaguered garrison at Kut before it surrendered on the 29th.

Initially declared as "missing", it was not until October that his parents were notified that he had in fact been killed. His remains were interred at the Amara War Cemetery where he receives his official commemoration.

BOWLES, H.

ARTHUR WILLIAM BOWLES

Whilst the identification of this man cannot be confirmed absolutely, there is compelling evidence to suggest that this name on the memorial is likely to be a commemoration of Arthur William Bowles. Strenuous attempts to find a match for the "H" Bowles named on the engraved memorial plate found no positive result, and there is no record of a "Bowles" with that initial having been present in the parish when the 1911 Census had been conducted. In addition, of the 15 men identified by the Commonwealth War Graves Commission as having lost their lives in the Great War who did have that combination of first initial and surname, none were found to have any obvious links with this area.

It was, however, the 1911 Census which showed that there was only one person present in the parish at that time who actually had this surname. Declared on that census return simply as Arthur Bowles, the additional information given on this document confirms that he was then 18 years of age and had been born in Fairford, Gloucestershire. A search of birth registration records for the entire county of Gloucestershire between March 1890 and December 1896 revealed only one suitable match for an Arthur William Bowles, who had his birth recorded in the September ¼ of 1892 at Cirencester. This larger town actually lies almost 9 miles away from Fairford, though the latter still falls within the boundaries of that larger registration district.

Further work was then undertaken with the records of both the Commonwealth War Graves Commission and "Soldiers Died...." which revealed that an Arthur William Bowles, who had been born in Cirencester, lost his life on the 1st day of the Battle of the Somme. Crucially, additional information held by the former also showed that his mother had been a *"Mrs. E. Bowles, of Cornwell, Oxford."* Taking this further, an examination of the Army Register of Soldiers Effects revealed that she was not only his sole legatee, but that her full first name had been Elizabeth. It is only by turning to the earlier census of 1901 however, that we are finally able to connect all these various threads together, by finding an entry for the then 8-year-old Arthur Bowles who was living with his father Albert and mother Elizabeth at Cornwell.

All of the above therefore proves that the Arthur William Bowles that is shown as a resident of Sutton-cum-Duckmanton in 1911 is the same man who lost his life in the Great War, and whilst no such links have been found for any "H. Bowles", they have thus been established for him. The final strands of evidence which confirm that this identification is likely to be correct actually came from both the original inscription on the memorial and the tablet in St Mary's Church at Sutton Scarsdale, both of which clearly give his initial as "A".

During 1911 Arthur was an estate worker employed at Sutton Scarsdale Hall with his occupation there listed as *"Dog Breaker"*. At that date, he was lodging with the East family in a property close to the Hall, and it is interesting to note that the children in that family had all been born in Cornwell. This may perhaps indicate that the East and Bowles families had much older associations, therefore making it plausible that, if this family had still been present in the district after the war, it was they who had remembered Arthur and put his name forward for inclusion on the memorial.

Dating Arthur's enlistment has proved very difficult using his 16942 service number, as other men that were issued with similar numbers by this regiment display a wide variety of different attestation dates. The only conclusion that can be drawn is that he seems most likely to have joined the army at some point between the 8th and 14th December 1915. By this date the flood of volunteers that had answered the original call to raise the units of Lord

Kitchener's "New Armies" had largely dried up, forcing the government to consider the introduction of conscription. Though some had favoured the adoption of this measure even in the days before war had been declared, there still remained, however, even at this late date, a widespread reluctance to introduce any form of enforced military service in Britain.

Frequently referred to as the "Derby Scheme" after its founder Lord Derby, the more correctly titled "Group Scheme" was a last attempt to persuade men to volunteer for military service of their own free will. It offered some flexibility to those who came forward to serve in the army, and allowed them the option to either defer until they were called or join the Colours immediately. Consequently, the total potential manpower generated by this initiative was split into 2 groups that were categorised as "A" and "B" respectively. Those who chose the option to defer were however still enlisted, but returned to their civilian occupations until they were mobilised to join their units. These men would then be called according to factors that considered a combination of both their ages and marital status, ensuring that the younger single men were mobilised ahead of their older married counterparts. To a limited extent, the volunteers of the Group Scheme were also allowed to express a preference regarding the units that they joined; something which would later be denied to those who were conscripted after the introduction of the Military Service Act. The scheme, however, largely came to be viewed as a failure, because large numbers of the men that were eligible simply failed to register for it.

The date of Arthur's enlistment makes it extremely likely that he volunteered under the Derby scheme, though we do not know if he attested for immediate service or opted to defer until he was called. In reality, it perhaps made little difference, because the combined factors of his young age and single status would have put him into one of the earliest groups to be mobilised.

The 9th (Service) Battalion of the Devonshire Regiment was originally formed entirely from volunteers during September 1914, and after landing at Le Havre in July 1915, became a unit of 20th Brigade in the 7th Division during early August. We can, however, be certain that Arthur, because he did not qualify for the 1914-15 Star, joined them at some point during 1916 as part of a reinforcement draft. We also know that he was with this unit on 1st July 1916 when they were involved in the infamous first day of the Somme Offensive.

Much has been written about this series of battles that raged across this sector of the Western Front between 1st July and 18th November 1916, with a great deal of the emphasis placed on that fateful first day. Widely acknowledged as the blackest day in British military history, it is perhaps easy enough to understand why that should be the case. Those who would seek a better understanding of this complex series of engagements would be best advised to read widely, taking into account the reasons why these battles were fought, how this chiefly British offensive fitted into the wider context of the Anglo-French alliance, and to assess the true impact that it had on an enemy that did not launch one single offensive anywhere on the Western Front during the whole of the following year.

At 07:30 hrs on 1st July the 9th Devons climbed out of their front line trench in Mametz Wood and began to cross no-mans-land to secure their objective, the village of Mametz itself. One of their officers, Captain Duncan Martin, had predicted that his men would come under heavy fire from a machine gun that the Germans had placed in the civilian cemetery opposite their starting position, and his prophecy sadly proved to be correct. The chattering fire from this gun cut a swathe through their ranks as the battalion advanced, and it is extremely likely that Arthur was one of its many victims. With the support of the 8th battalion of the same regiment, however, the Devon's drove home their attack and successfully secured the hotly contested village.

After the battle, the bodies of the fallen were brought back across no-mans-land and buried in the same front-line trench from which their attack had started, thus creating what is known to this day as the Devonshire Cemetery at Mametz. Some short time afterwards a wooden cross was erected there which perhaps bore one of the most powerful and poignant epitaphs that can be found anywhere on the Western Front, it simply read:

The Devonshires held this trench. The Devonshires hold it still.

In addition to his official commemoration at this cemetery and the likelihood of his being remembered at Sutton-cum-Duckmanton and Sutton Scarsdale, Arthur is also remembered on the memorials in the villages of Bratton Clovelly in Devon and Cornwell in Oxfordshire.

WARDLE, T.

JOHN EDWARD WARDLE

 Regrettably, this identification highlights another spelling error on the memorial, as both the original stone inscription and the memorial at St. Mary's Church list him as "Wardle, J. E.". In addition, none of the 13 men shown on the records of the Commonwealth War Graves Commission that could have been described as "Wardle, T" have any obvious association with the local district. The same, however, is not true of 17771, Pte. John Edward Wardle, who lost his life on 4th July 1916 whilst serving with the 10th (Service) Battalion of the Sherwood Foresters. The most compelling evidence in support of this identification, however, comes from the fact that Albert Henry Wardle, who is now remembered on the memorial as "Wardle, A.", was his brother. In what was set to become a double tragedy for the family, he would lose his life just over a year after John, whilst serving with the same battalion of the regiment. In an obituary published for Albert, mention is actually made that he had *"lost one brother in the war"*, although this source unfortunately fails to name him.

The 1901 Census shows the family to have been living in Poolsbrook at that date, and clearly details that Albert Henry and John Edward were brothers who were then aged 12 and 7 respectively. It further informs us that their parents were Joseph (aged 43) and Emily (aged 41), and that both the father and his 2 sons had been born at Ilkeston. This location for the birth of the brothers is in fact further confirmed by their respective entries within "Soldiers Died...."

The later 1911 Census shows us that the previous decade had brought great changes for the Wardle family, and with the death of

Emily having been recorded later in 1901, Joseph is shown in 1911 with a new wife named Edith. John Edward was still living with this family at this date, who were then residing at 48, Mafeking Terrace, Spital Lane, Chesterfield. A 1911 Census entry for his brother Albert Henry, however, shows that he was then living in Mansfield Woodhouse, as a lodger in the household of a Henry Lilleman.

Further links for Joseph and Edith to the parish of Sutton-cum-Duckmanton also come from 2 other sources. Firstly, the Army's Register of Soldiers Effects entry for Albert Henry records the names of both his father and step-mother. Secondly, his entry in the records of the Commonwealth War Graves Commission declares him to have been the *"Son of Joseph Wardle, of 99, Arkwright Town, Chesterfield."* His father and step-mother must therefore have moved to Arkwright at some point after the 1911 Census was taken. The same Register of Soldiers Effects also tells us that John Edward had been married, as it names his sole legatee as his widow "Sarah A.", and a marriage registration recorded in the Chesterfield district during the June ¼ of 1912 supports this by confirming that John Edward Wardle had married Sarah A. Morgan.

On Saturday 22nd July 1916, the Derbyshire Courier carried a full page of casualty portraits, amongst which is the one shown here for J. E. Wardle. This links him to Clay Cross at the time of his death and, as he is also remembered on the memorial outside their parish church, it seems likely that he had moved into that district around the time of his marriage. In another obituary for him that was printed in the Derbyshire Times on 15th July 1916, we are told that, whilst he had at one time been employed at Markham Colliery, he had actually been working at Grassmoor Colliery just before he enlisted. This other obituary also gives us an even greater insight into his death and family connections. It begins with the statement *"News has been received at 99, Arkwright Town by the parents of Private John E. Wardle that their son was killed in action on July 3rd."* Before going on to state that *"The first intimation was received from Albert, another soldier son of Mr and Mrs Wardle."* Stunningly, Albert's own words are then quoted from that letter.

"All his chums wish me to forward to you their sympathy, and to tell you that he died doing his bit, for he was in the thick of the

fight. He died instantly. I was not far away at the time, but I could not get to see him. He will be put away comfortably with many other good lads. His chums will get their own back. We are out to win, and shall win."

Further evidence from the Chesterfield register of births, marriages and deaths supplies us with the additional information that John and his wife had 2 children, one of whom, a son that was also named "John E.", had been born at around the time of his father's death.

From his service number, we know that John probably enlisted on or around 5th October 1914, and we can see from his Medal Roll entries and Medal Index Card that he landed in France when the whole of the 10th (Service) Battalion began their overseas service on the 14th July 1915. This unit was the 2nd "Service" battalion to be raised by the regiment, and was a part of Lord Kitchener's 2nd "New Army". Forming a part of 51st Brigade within the 17th (Northern) Division, they were originally deployed to Belgium in the southern part of the Ypres Salient, and suffered heavy casualties there in February of 1916 defending a position known as "The Bluff". No reports have, however, been found to indicate that John was ever placed on any casualty list prior to his death.

The Battalion later moved into the infamous Somme sector of the front to play a role in the major offensive that was launched there on 1st July 1916. Though they were not directly involved in the disastrous events of that first day, they were called into action the following day to support an attack being made on the village of Fricourt. They made good steady progress both that day and on the 3rd, when despite running into German opposition, they managed to both gain ground and hold onto it. Withdrawn from the line by midday on the 4th, their fatal casualties had been comparatively light with just 13 men killed and a further 8 missing. As they marched away to their camp at Ville, however, John was no longer with them.

Sadly, whilst Albert had assured his parents that John's body would rest amongst those of his fallen comrades, his remains were either subsequently lost or could not later be identified. He therefore receives his official commemoration on the memorial to the missing of the Somme at Thiepval. Bearing silent witness to the huge sacrifices that were made on this sector of the Western Front during the Great War, this monument is the largest of those cared for by the Commonwealth War Graves Commission. It records the names of over 72,000 men that have no known grave and who lost their lives there before 20th March 1918.

The memorial to the missing of the Somme at Thiepval.

BANTON, C.

CHARLES PERCIVAL BANTON

The birth of Charles Banton was recorded in the Derby district during the December ¼ of 1892, and he is shown on the 1901 Census (at the age of 8), as the son of Bricklayer's Labourer John Banton and his wife Anne. Additional information from the later 1911 Census shows us that he was actually born in Mickleover. By that date, however, he was living as a boarder in the household of the Gascoyne family at 136, Speedwell Terrace, Staveley, and was employed as a *"Coal Mine Pony Driver"*.

From the evidence provided by his entry in the Register of Soldiers Effects, we discover that his Widow, "Gertrude A. A." is recorded as his sole legatee. There is actually only one matching marriage record to be found in the whole of the county and, registered in the Derby district during the September ¼ of 1913, it is this source which reveals that his wife's maiden name had been Roe.

It would seem that Charles' return to Derby was only a temporary affair, as subsequent birth records demonstrate that the couple went on to have 3 sons (Charles in 1914, George in 1915, and Arnold in 1916), all of whom had their births registered in the Chesterfield district. His obituary in the Derbyshire Times fortunately confirms that his wife was living at 22, Arkwright Town when the sad news of his death reached her, and therefore provides the solid connection to the parish that was needed to bring certainty to his identification. We are also able to see from the same registration database that Gertrude would go on to remarry in Derby during the early months of 1921, becoming Mrs Walter J. Ashmole.

With neither pension nor service records surviving for Charles, we have to look at other sources to gain some knowledge about his time in the army. When we turn to his obituary for more detail, however, we are presented with one piece of information that completely conflicts with what survives in the remnants of the official records. It states that he first enlisted with the "K.O.R.L.R." or King's Own Royal Lancaster Regiment. Whilst the records of the Commonwealth War Graves Commission provide no personal details, Charles' entry in "Soldiers Died…." confirms that he was born in Derby and had enlisted in Chesterfield. Both of these sources, however, also confirm that his service number with the Notts & Derby Regiment had been 17453, which indicates that his service with them had begun on either the 28th or 29th September 1914. Unless he had a very rapid transfer to the Sherwood Foresters, which is most unlikely, the mention of the K.O.R.L.R. in his obituary would seem to be an error. On consulting the Medal Rolls we can also determine that he initially landed in France on 29th August 1915 along with the whole of the 12th (Service) Battalion of the Notts & Derby Regiment, and that at some later date he was transferred to their 2nd Regular Army battalion. There is in fact no other evidence to be found anywhere of him ever having served overseas with any regiment but the Foresters.

The timing of Charles' enlistment actually makes it extremely likely that he was a "founder member" of the 12th (Service) Battalion, which was raised in Derby as a unit for Lord Kitchener's 3rd "New Army" on the 1st October 1914. Originally envisaged as a fighting unit for the newly forming 24th Division, they were moved to Shoreham for their training. Circumstances at the front, with the war having by then evolved into one of static trench warfare, brought about a change to this original plan, and in April of 1915 they were converted into a specialist "Pioneer" Battalion for their Division. This meant that they were not assigned to serve within a Brigade, which at this period was a formation composed of 4 infantry battalions, but were instead designated as Divisional Troops. As such, they would be deployed at Divisional rather than Brigade level, and be sent to the forward areas where the need for their specialised skills was the greatest. They had, amongst other things, a key role in consolidating positions captured or defended by the infantry, and in keeping the ever-growing network of trenches in a good state of repair. They were, however, still very much a front-line fighting unit, and in times of need could also be called upon to fulfil that role too.

Whilst we are unable to determine Charles' transfer date from the 12th to the 2nd Battalion, his obituary states that he was invalided home with rheumatic fever shortly after his arrival and did not return to France until January of 1916. In addition to this, a notice was also printed in the Sheffield Daily Telegraph on 26th May 1916 which reported *"Sherwood Foresters – Banton 17453 C. (Chesterfield)"* as *"Wounded, Shock-Shell"*. This therefore allows us to speculate that either of these interruptions in his active service could have marked the end of his time with the 12th Battalion. At the time that the newspaper report appeared in the Sheffield paper, the 24th Division was in the Southern part of the Ypres Salient near Wulverghem, where the Germans had recently released huge clouds of poison gas.

The 2nd Battalion of the Notts & Derby Regiment were serving on the right side of the British sector of the Somme Offensive during August 1916, close to the river Ancre, and in front of the heavily defended German positions at Beaumont Hamel. During this period they took no part in the major offensive, but were involved in holding a section of the front line with all the attendant risks that this entailed. One of the more onerous tasks that the battalion undertook during a tour of the trenches that lasted from 5th to 11th August, was the recovery and burial of the dead that had resulted from the previous heavy fighting in the vicinity. On being relieved, their diary records that 15 of their men had been wounded during this tour, chiefly by German artillery fire, and it is therefore likely that Charles was amongst them.

The entry for Charles in "Soldiers Died…." unambiguously states that he died from wounds, and the use of this specific terminology tells us that, having been injured by the enemy, he had entered the casualty clearing system before his death. In cases like this, it is always useful to consult the information available from the Commonwealth War Graves Commission concerning the history of the cemetery where men were laid to rest and receive their official commemorations. In this instance, their historical notes for Heilly Station Cemetery at Merricourt L'Abbe inform us that the 36th, 38th and 2/2nd Casualty Clearing Stations were all in the vicinity when Charles, at the age of 23, succumbed to his injuries on 9th August 1916. His obituary provides a little further information on this by publishing the contents of a letter sent to Gertrude by Canon R. E. Adderley. He stated that:

"I am very sorry to tell you that your husband, Pte C. P. Banton, passed away last night. We were hoping he would have pulled through, but God has willed otherwise. During his Illness he received my ministrations most gratefully, and died a good soldier of Jesus Christ. I buried him this evening in Heilly Military Cemetery. Please accept my deep sympathy in your sad loss."

Originally named on both the stonework of the memorial and the tablet in St. Mary's Church as "C. BANTAM", unfortunately, his name was missed altogether from the engraved metal plates that were added to the former after the end of the Second World War. In its place, however, the name of "C. BARBER" mysteriously appeared in what is thought to have been a simple transcription error. In more recent times this has been corrected, and though Banton's name has now been added, that of Barber has not correspondingly been removed. All of the surviving paperwork consistently gives this man's surname as "BANTON" rather than "BANTAM", and when his name was finally added to the memorial the spelling used that format.

WEBB, W.

WILLIAM JOSEPH WARREN WEBB

 Whilst the obituary printed in the Derbyshire Times for William provided some details about him, it actually revealed very little about his early life. We therefore had to seek out his entry in "Soldiers Died...." to discover that he had been born in the village of Farthingstone. Located in rural Northamptonshire, about 10 miles to the West of the county town, this settlement falls under the area covered by the Daventry registration district where a record was made for his birth during the June ¼ of 1882.

His entry in the Army Registers of Soldiers' Effects confirms that William's next of kin was his mother, who it names as Mary M. Bucknell. Whilst their surnames are obviously not the same, this is, however, consistent with details found in his obituary which mention that the official news of his death had been received by a Mrs Bucknell at 106, Arkwright Town. The entries on the 1911 Census add little to our knowledge, but do confirm that Mary Maria Bucknell was then living at that address with her husband William Bucknell. William Webb, on the other hand, was actually living as a boarder at another address in Arkwright Town just a few doors away. Whilst the earlier 1901 Census shows William living with Mary and William Bucknell at an address in Calow, he is confusingly described as being a nephew rather than a son or step-son. With recourse to the registration data, we can, however, gain a clearer understanding of William's family. These records confirm that the wedding of William Bucknell and Mary Maria Webb had taken place in the Daventry district of Northamptonshire during the September ¼ of 1894, and that her earlier marriage to James Joseph Webb (under her maiden name of Gilkes) had taken place in that same district during the December ¼ of 1881.

William's obituary fills in several more gaps by informing us that he had been working at Markham No1 Colliery for almost 20 years prior to his enlistment. This, therefore, makes it likely that he had moved to this area circa 1896. It also informs us that he had enlisted into the Lincolnshire Regiment in May 1915, whilst other records show that it is most likely to have been in the final days of that month, between the 29th-31st, and that this had occurred in Chesterfield.

In the absence of surviving service or pension records we cannot say for certain where he received his basic training, though this is most likely to have been delivered by either the 3rd (Reserve) Battalion at Grimsby or the 9th (Reserve) Battalion at Lincoln. We do, however, know that all of his overseas service was with the 6th (Service) Battalion of the regiment and that, as this was raised in Lincoln during August 1914, he could not have been one of their original members. This is further evidenced by the fact that the 6th Battalion had begun its overseas service in Gallipoli during July 1915, whilst William had not joined it until December of that year. There is, however, some confusion surrounding where his overseas service with it actually began, because whilst his Medal Index Card clearly shows that he started his journey to the Balkan theatre of war on 12th December, the 11th (Northern) Division was actually withdrawn from the Gallipoli peninsula to the neighbouring island of Imbros on 19th/20th of that month, and did not continue on to Egypt until late January / early February 1916. His obituary, however, clearly states that he was "...drafted to Egypt where he landed on Boxing Day." It would therefore seem more likely that he landed in Alexandria and had stayed at a Depot there until, in effect, his new unit joined him.

Like the 9th Battalion of the Sherwood Foresters, the 6th Battalion of the Lincolns was the first "Service" battalion to be raised by that regiment and, as these 2 units were both members of the 33rd Brigade of the 11th (Northern) Division, they fought side by side for the entire duration of the war.

Once arrived in Egypt, the 6th Lincolns were deployed on the defences of the Suez Canal, and this was actually a quiet time for them, where the opportunity was taken to consolidate and rest after the rigours of the Gallipoli campaign. Based at Sidi Bashr adjacent to Alexandria, there is much surviving evidence to show that the men of the 11th Division had sufficient leisure time to swim in the Nile or even make trips to visit the Pyramids. The only glimpse we are afforded of William's time here comes from his obituary, and speaks of his apparent satisfaction at leaving both the heat and desert sand behind him when they were re-deployed to the Somme region of France in July 1916.

William would have sailed into the harbour at Marseilles with the rest of his battalion aboard the troop ship "Huntspill" on 8th July, and though they had therefore missed the horrors of the first day of the Somme Offensive, they would have a far from easy time in the months that lay ahead. Perhaps one of the most notable events that William would have witnessed was the Battle of Flers Courcellete in September, where tanks were used for the first time in the history of warfare.

Unfortunately, some mystery surrounds William's loss, though there are some clues to be found in the surviving documentation. His obituary refers to him as having *"died from gunshot wounds in the arms and leg received accidentally on September 24th."* This is backed by his entry in "Soldiers Died...." which gives his cause of death as "Died." This categorisation, whilst at first appearing to be most unhelpful, was actually reserved for those who had lost their lives in circumstances which could not be directly attributed to any action by the enemy. The War Diary, however, makes no mention of any casualties between the 19th–26th September, except for detailing that one fatality had occurred on the 25th. For this it simply records *"One OR killed in Aveluy carrying ammunition."* The date of William's death, however, is shown by both the Commonwealth War Graves Commission and "Soldiers Died...." as having occurred on the previous day. Another of their men, named Will Booth, who is buried at Aveluy, however, is shown as having died on the 25th, and it must therefore be assumed that this entry in the Battalion War Diary relates to him.

William is buried at Contay British Cemetery, which lies about 10 miles to the West of Aveluy beside the main road between Amiens and Arras, and we know that he must have succumbed to his wounds at either the 9th or 49th Casualty Clearing Stations as both of these units were based in this area at the time. His only known commemorations in the Chesterfield district are on the memorials at Sutton-cum-Duckmanton and at St. Mary's Church in Sutton

Scarsdale, both of which originally recorded his surname as "WEBBE". They are, however, the only sources we have found which use that spelling variation.

COE, G.

GEORGE E. COE

George, who had his birth registered in the Chesterfield district during the March ¼ of 1893, was the son of George and Elizabeth Ann (Case) who had married in that same district during 1887. Though his father had originated from the small village of North Lopham in Southern Norfolk, his mother was a local girl from Calow Green.

The 1901 Census shows the family living at 8, Arkwright Town when George was just an 8-year-old schoolboy, and his parents were still at that same address when the tragic news of his death reached them in the spring of 1917. At the age of 18, the 1911 Census shows us that, like his father, George was working in the local mining industry where his occupation was quite precisely defined as *"Colliery Screen Labourer Above – working on pit bank."* A line in his obituary further confirms that, before he had enlisted in January 1915, he had been employed at Markham No2 pit, whilst from another line in this same source we also know that he had been a keen Cricketer in his leisure time.

Interestingly, a note found on his record in "Soldiers Died...." states that George first enlisted into the Sherwood Foresters, who had originally issued him with the service number 3696. We also know, from the evidence of the Medal Rolls and his Medal Index Card, that George's only overseas service was with the Machine Gun Corps, and that this had commenced at some point after the 31st December 1915.

Owing to the lack of surviving records, we are unable to be certain about the details of George's initial service with the Sherwood Foresters, though we are able to give an approximate date for the issue of his 46558 service number with the Machine Gun Corps.

The numbers in this series were being issued between the end of July and the beginning of August 1916, and he must therefore have transferred to his new unit at that date. This also indicates the earliest date that he could have seen his first overseas service would have been in the later months of that same year.

It is worthwhile giving some information here concerning the Machine Gun Corps, as they were formed as a direct result of experience gained from Britain's involvement in the early months of the Great War. Comparatively short-lived, they came into being on 22nd October 1915 and were disbanded in 1922. The importance of their role, however, should not be overlooked. A total of 170,500 men served with them during the war, of which over 62,000 were either killed, wounded, or declared as missing. Suffering such a high mortality rate, it was not for nothing that they came to be known amongst the ordinary Tommies of the infantry battalions as "The Suicide Club."

At the beginning of hostilities, each infantry battalion had its own Machine Gun Section equipped with 2 Maxim guns that were each capable of firing 500 rounds per minute. After early clashes with their enemies, however, it quickly became recognised in the British Expeditionary Force that better use could be made of these weapons if they were grouped together en-masse, and in early 1915 the number of machine guns per section was doubled to four. Taking this concept a stage further, with the creation of the Machine Gun Corps, all of the existing machine gun sections were withdrawn from their individual battalions and grouped into a Company that would serve all four battalions within their Brigade. This approach still allowed for the guns to be deployed individually, but with greater care taken to ensure that they had interlocking fields of fire. There were other developments too, as it was also realised that machine guns could be used like artillery. Not only could they be aimed in a high arc to hit targets on the far side of hills and other obstacles on the battlefield "indirectly", but they were also capable of providing an impenetrable curtain of fire similar to that produced by an artillery barrage.

As a member of the 197th Company of the Corps, George would almost certainly have been trained at Grantham and gone out to join the 9th (Scottish) Division in December 1916. His obituary records that George suffered severe internal injuries from the bursting of a shrapnel shell on 10th April 1917, at which time the 9th Division were involved in an action that was being fought during the opening stages of the Arras offensive which would later be known as the First Battle of The Scarpe. Evacuated to No7 Canadian General Hospital at Etaples, he succumbed to these injuries the following day at the age of 24. A Nurse from that Hospital, identified in his obituary as P. E. Roberts, was with him at the end and wrote to communicate the sad news to his parents. His obituary tells us that, amongst other items that she had sent with her letter, there was also a diary in which George had recorded all of his experiences during his time in the army.

He receives his official commemoration at his final resting place in the Etaples Military Cemetery, and his name is only recorded locally on the memorials at Sutton-cum-Duckmanton and Sutton Scarsdale.

HORNER, W.

WALTER ERNEST HORNER

 Walter is quite an unusual casualty, because he did not actually serve in the British army. He was killed at the age of 30 as a member of the Australian Imperial Force, whilst serving in France with their 11th Infantry Battalion. His identity may actually have remained a mystery had it not been for a brief note in the records of the Commonwealth War Graves Commission which states that he was the *"Son of John and Mary Ann Horner, of Upper Vann Farm, Hambledon, Godalming, Surrey, England. Born at Scarsdale, Derbyshire, England."* A search of the birth registration records confirmed that an entry was made for him in the Chesterfield district during the December ¼ of 1888, and the 1911 Census also confirms a lot of detail for us by showing that, at that later date, the then 22-year-old Walter was still living with his parents at Nursery Farm in Calow. His father, despite being 70 years old during that census year, was working as an Institute Caretaker, whilst Walter was employed in the local mining industry as a *"Colliery Labourer Above Ground."* Though neither of his parents were born locally, they had obviously lived in the area for a number of years, and evidence from the registration data shows that they had married in the Chesterfield district during 1881.

With his parents having moved to Godalming at some point after the 1911 Census had been conducted, it would have been very easy for Walter's connection to the parish to have been severed and his name not put forward for inclusion on the memorial. Evidence from both the 1901 Census and the register of marriages, however, shows that at least one of his siblings married in the Chesterfield district, and it is therefore likely that they had remained in the area to remember him here after his parents had moved away. It also seems likely that Walter had left for Australia at the end of October 1914, as a man of the correct age named as Walter E. Horner has been found on the passenger list of a ship named the "Ophir" which departed from London for Freemantle.

Australian historians and genealogists are much more fortunate than we are in Britain, because all of the service records of their soldiers from the Great War have survived. In Walter's case, these documents reveal that he enlisted at Perth in Western Australia on 7th September 1915 at the age of 27 years and 11 months, giving his occupation as *"Yardman"*. He actually declared on his attestation forms that he had tried to enlist the previous February, but on that occasion, the Army had rejected him because he was suffering from sunburn!

The subsequent pages of his records show us that after completing his training he began the long journey to the European theatre of war via Suez, Alexandria, Marseilles, and the Infantry Base Depot at Etaples, where he arrived on 9th April 1916. From there, he joined the 11th Infantry Battalion in the field on 25th May as a member of their 13th reinforcement draft. At that date, they were in the vicinity of Sailly Sur La Lys which lies midway between Bethune and Armentieres.

The 11th Infantry Battalion was a wartime raised unit and was therefore the Australian equivalent of a "Service" battalion in the British army. It was actually the first battalion to be raised in Western Australia, and its original members had already fought against the Turks in Gallipoli before being re-deployed to France.

After the opening of the Somme offensive on 1st July 1916, the battalion was re-deployed to Albert on the 19th of that month, and was soon engaged in heavy fighting at Pozieres. Walter was seriously wounded on or around 22nd August when the unit was taking part in an attack at Mouquet Farm. The injuries that he received there are recorded as shrapnel wounds to both the right thigh and left shoulder, and they were considered to be so severe that he was evacuated through the casualty clearing system before finally being admitted to Edmonton Military Hospital in England on 29th August.

He did not return to France until 4th December, and did not actually rejoin his unit in the field near Fleurs until Boxing Day. He was only there briefly, however, before being admitted to hospital again on 12th January 1917, this time suffering from inflammation of his feet. Returning to his unit again on 2nd February, he would then serve with them continuously until he was reported missing on 16th April. By which date, the battalion was at Louverval in support of the southern edge of the Arras Offensive. On the 15th April, they had been involved in repelling a large German raid that later became known as the Battle of Lagnicourt, for his part in which their Lieutenant Charles Pope was later awarded a posthumous VC. It is extremely likely that Walter was one of the men killed during a desperate charge that this officer led to prevent the Germans from capturing the ground that they had been instructed to hold at all costs. Initially declared as missing, it would not actually be until a court of enquiry was held on 5th December that it was officially accepted that he had in fact been killed.

Walter's remains were either never found or could not be identified, and he therefore receives his official commemoration at the Villers-Bretonneux Memorial. This monument is actually the Australian National Memorial, erected to commemorate all those who fought in both France and Belgium during the course of the Great War. His only commemorations in the Chesterfield district are at Sutton-cum-Duckmanton and Sutton Scarsdale.

BARBER, W.

WILLIAM BARBER

 William Barber is buried in the cemetery beside what was formerly St Peter's and St Paul's Church on Rectory Road in Duckmanton. The local connections of this man were, therefore, obvious from the outset because, after the early months of 1915, it became possible for the remains of any British servicemen who had died in the UK to be sent back to his home parish for burial. Further evidence, however, is to be found in the records of the Commonwealth War Graves Commission which declare him to have been the *"Son of James and Selina Barber, of 142, Arkwright Town, Chesterfield. Born at Duckmanton."*

Tracking the family back on the 1911 Census we find them in the parish, and discover that at the age of 19 William was employed at one of the local collieries as a Blacksmith's Striker. As we have his age at death recorded by the Commonwealth War Graves Commission at 26, we can also be reasonably certain that the record of William's birth was the one for his name that was registered in the Chesterfield district during the June ¼ of 1891.

With no surviving service or pension records, we must look to other sources in order to determine something of William's time in the army. In turning to these other documents, we discover that he served with the 9th (Service) Battalion of the Sherwood Foresters with a service number of 12902, which dates his attestation to 18th August 1914, and therefore makes him a very early wartime volunteer. The 9th was the first "Service" battalion that the regiment raised for Lord Kitchener's first "New Army", and hold the distinction of being the only battalion of the Foresters ever to have served in the ill-fated Gallipoli campaign. Further evidence from

William's Medal Index Card not only shows that he served with them in that theatre of operations, but that he had almost certainly been promoted to the rank of Corporal before he left England.

The 9th (Service) Battalion were raised at Derby during August of 1914, and would later see service as a unit of the 33rd Brigade within the 11th (Northern) Division. The first batches of volunteers that served with it were actually housed under canvas in Markeaton Park, and the finding of more suitable accommodation for what was destined to become a 1,000 strong fighting force was therefore amongst the first of many logistical obstacles that they would be required to overcome. Alternative arrangements were however soon made, and as each Company was formed, they were moved out to Belton Park near Grantham where a dedicated camp was set up for them in purpose built wooden huts.

The 9th next moved to Frensham in Surrey during April of 1915, and on 1st July were embarked at Liverpool for their voyage to Alexandria. They were not destined to stay very long in this Egyptian port however, before another much shorter sailing took them on to the island of Mudros. Located just off the Gallipoli peninsula, they arrived there at a time when preparations were already in hand for a large-scale landing on the mainland. The battalion was, however, next sent to the Southern tip of the Gallipoli peninsular to gain some experience in the trenches there before being shipped to Imbros, another small island in closer proximity to the West of their intended landing zone on the mainland.

Going ashore at Suvla Bay on 7th August, the battalion initially met with very little resistance. This however, was set to change just 2 days later when, whilst taking part in a major advance, it encountered a well-trained and determined Turkish force in the vicinity of a geographical feature known as Chocolate Hill. It was in an orchard beside this landmark that the 9th Battalion fought its first battle and suffered a high number of casualties. From a surviving article that was published in the Derbyshire Times on 19th May 1917 concerning his death, we know that William was with them on that fateful day. The level of detail given in this press coverage provides so much additional information, and fills so many other gaps in our knowledge, that it is reproduced here in full:

"Mr and Mrs J. Barber of Nursery House, Arkwright Town, received a telegram on Tuesday last from the Commandant of Sandon Hospital, Staffordshire, conveying the sad news of the death of their son, Sergt. W. Barber, 12902. Mrs Barber immediately journeyed to Sandon and learned that her son lost his life through boating alone in an old disused boat in the moat in the hospital grounds. The body was not recovered until the dragging operations had been proceeded with for an hour and a half."

"An inquest was held on Wednesday, the verdict being "Accidentally Drowned." The coffin was conveyed from Oxley Station to Chesterfield by rail, thence by road to Arkwright Town, arriving at Nursery House at 8:30 the same evening. The interment took place on Friday at the Duckmanton burial ground."

"Sergt. W. Barber volunteered for active service at the commencement of the war, joining the Notts. and Derby. Regiment on August 18th 1914. Whilst engaged in a severe attack in the Dardanelles on August 9th, 1915, he received a nasty bullet wound to the wrist. After receiving treatment at the Military Hospital, Malta, he was invalided home to Colchester. About a year ago he was ordered to Sandon Hospital to take charge of a Company of convalescent soldiers."

"Before joining up Sergt. Barber was employed as a Blacksmith at Markham Colliery, and was a great favourite with all who knew him. He was a valuable member of the Duckmanton Church Choir, and a thorough sportsman, a keen tennis player and cricketer. Had he lived until Wednesday last he would have been 26 years of age."

As with all the other men remembered on the parish memorial, his was a life cut short in the service of his country, and a later article published on 26th May gives fuller coverage of his funeral. This states that full military honours were accorded, and that the firing party was made up of volunteers from the Chesterfield district under the command of Lieut. J. Heath.

IND, W.

WILLIAM ERNEST IND

We were provided with a wealth of information about William in a large and detailed obituary that was printed for him in the Derbyshire Times on 16th June 1917. To discover something of his early life, however, still required an examination of the civil registration data and Census returns.

The census for 1911 shows a 19-year-old William living with his siblings and parents at an address that was simply given as *"Duckmanton School – Chesterfield."* This is something that is readily explained by the occupation of his father, which was declared as *"Elementary School Teacher – Derbyshire County Council."*

Turning the clock back to 1890 shows that his parents, William Herbert and Martha Ann (Griffiths), had their marriage recorded in the Shropshire town of Oswestry during the December ¼ of that year, and we also find that the registration of William's birth took place in that same district during the same ¼ of the following year. We know that his father had been Schoolmaster and Organist at Duckmanton since 1903, and so William would have been around 12 years old when his family first moved into the parish. We also know that from then until 1909 he was a student at Chesterfield Grammar School, and that he is also remembered on their memorial. A keen sportsman and obviously a bright lad, before William left school he had passed the London Intermediate Examinations and later followed this up by sitting the exams for entry into the Second Division Clerkships of the Civil Service.

Success here saw him placed in the Scottish Education Department before being offered a permanent appointment on the Local Government Board.

William enlisted into the Territorial Force before the war, becoming a member of the 1st/15th (County of London) Battalion (Prince of Wales's Own Civil Service Rifles). This was one of the twenty-eight battalions of the County of London Regiment, which should not be confused with the City of London Regiment that was a completely different unit of the Regular Army. His obituary mentions those pre-war days and paints a picture of William as a model soldier. His marksmanship is described as being *"little short of perfect"*, so good in fact that he had won the "D" Company's Cup for two years in succession. The battalion that he joined was originally based at Somerset House, but moved to Bedmond in Hertfordshire when they were mobilised at the start of the hostilities, and was finally relocated to billets in nearby Watford during November 1914.

After war was declared, despite William then only holding the rank of Corporal, he soon began to be offered commissions in other regiments. His obituary, however, tells us that he turned down all of these opportunities, preferring to remain with his own battalion. This loyalty was eventually rewarded in February of the following year, when he was both offered and accepted a commission as a Second Lieutenant in his own unit. This appointment, however, was not confirmed in the London Gazette until the publication of their edition dated for 1st April 1915.

Grouped with other battalions from the London Regiment, William's unit landed at Le Havre on 18th March 1915 and served throughout the whole of the war in the 4th Brigade of the 47th (2nd London) Division. As with all the units of the Territorial Force, the members of this battalion had not originally been obliged to serve overseas unless they had additionally volunteered to do so, though we are told in his obituary that 95% of the men in this battalion actually made that extra commitment during the very month in which war had been declared. Though a very strong indicator of the commitment of these particular men, it should be noted that this level of enthusiasm was by no means unique to the 1st/15th London's.

His obituary informs us that William was *"slightly wounded in the arm in one of his first engagements."* Whilst he is not mentioned by name in the battalion's War Diary, this does make it possible that he was one of the 3 officers who were wounded on 25th May 1915 whilst his unit were supporting a successful attack on Givenchy, about 30 miles to the South West of Lille. The main thrust of this particular attack was, however, actually made by the 142nd Brigade who were in the line to the right of William's battalion. The next entry we find for him in the London Gazette appears on 14th January 1916, confirming that he had been made a temporary Lieutenant with effect from 24th September. His next step up the ladder of promotion would, however, come much more quickly, being confirmed in the London Gazette on 13th November of that same year when, and whilst already serving as Adjutant, he became a temporary Captain.

William's obituary goes on to give many more details, including a mention that the gallantry he had displayed on one occasion in leading up ammunition and other supplies to the battalion by night had resulted in him being awarded the Military Cross, the confirmation of which appeared on page 36 of the London Gazette dated for the 1st January 1917. The obituary also goes on to detail several of his other experiences stating that…

"He was also mentioned in dispatches after a later attack. On many occasions he volunteered to reconnoitre the various positions of the enemy, and consequently experienced hair breadth escapes."

"One evening he was compelled to lie for twenty minutes in the hollow at the foot of a German trench until the enemy ceased sending up star-shells. He crept back to his comrades unseen, conveying much valuable information. On another occasion whilst examining the intricate barbed wire arrangements of the enemy, our guns opened fire fifteen minutes before the time expected. He immediately dropped into a shell-hole and waited until the firing was over, many shells dropping within a few yards of him."

At some point during late April or early May of 1917, William was given acting rank as a Brigade Major. He would, however, be killed around one month later when he received what would prove to be a fatal wound on the 7th June, the first day of the Battle of Messines. On that date, his battalion was engaged in an attack which was part of the second phase of those operations, in the vicinity of a landmark known as White Chateau. Having gone forward to ensure that their advance was going well, William was struck on the head by a piece of shell. Initially it seems, judging from the tone of a letter written to his parents by Lieutenant Colonel William Newson that, despite the wound being described as serious, there were strong hopes that he would recover. William was sent back to No 10 Casualty Clearing Station near Poperinghe, but lost his struggle for life later on that same day without regaining consciousness. He was just 25 years old.

Describing his death as their *"most serious loss since leaving England"*, the official history produced by the regiment after the war goes on to state that he was *"the finest Territorial soldier who ever served with them"*, and that *"he was loved by every officer, N.C.O. and man in the battalion."* There is perhaps little doubt that, had he lived, William would have gone on to achieve greater things.

His remains were interred at Lijssenthoek Military Cemetery, where his headstone acts as his official commemoration. Despite this site containing over 9900 burials of men from Britain and her Empire who fell during the Great War, this is not the largest such cemetery to be found on the Western Front.

CUPITT, J.

JOHN CUPIT

An obituary was published for John in the Derbyshire Times and Chesterfield Herald on 4th August 1917. Though it provides little in the way of detail, it both confirms that he had been serving with the Sherwood Foresters and proves his connection with the parish by stating that, when she had received the news of his death, his wife had been living at 140, Arkwright Town.

Interestingly, like the memorial, the article uses the double "TT" spelling of his surname whilst several of the other contemporary records that have been found for him use the single "T" version. Fortunately, according to the Commonwealth War Graves Commission, only one man with either spelling of this surname and the initial "J" lost his life whilst serving with the Sherwood Foresters during the Great War, and they list him as 20528, Pte. John Cupit of the 12th Battalion. The date that they give for the death of this soldier, 26th July 1917, also fits neatly with the timing of the publication date for the obituary that had appeared in the Derbyshire Times. Sadly, his is one of many war graves records for the Great War era which neither gives his age nor any information about his family, making his obituary a vital source in determining his identity.

His entry in the Army Registers of Soldier's Effects reveals that his wife's Christian name was Olive, providing us with an additional clue that we can use to look at other sources in order to determine something of his background. A search of registration data for Derbyshire duly reveals that the marriage of a John Cupitt to an Olive Bewley had been recorded in the December ¼ of 1911 at Chesterfield. From his obituary, we also know that the couple had

"4 young children", and initially three of these could be identified quite readily. The places where their births were registered, however, show a wide degree of variation, implying that the family had moved quite regularly. The eldest of the three was Robert, B. who had his birth recorded in Chesterfield during the September ¼ of 1912. He was followed by John, who had his birth recorded in Pontefract during the December ¼ of 1914, and the youngest, George, R., had his birth recorded in Sheffield during the September ¼ of 1917.

Fortunately, some of the information we have about John from "Soldiers Died…." actually corroborates the location details for the birth registrations of his sons. In addition to telling us that he himself had been born in Tibshelf, it also informs us that John had enlisted at Pontefract and that he was actually residing in Castleford (which was within the Pontefract registration district) at the time of his enlistment.

Armed with enough information to search the census returns for 1911, we discover that at that date John and Olive were living in his native Tibshelf. We also, at last, discover the name of their eldest child, a daughter named Nora who is shown as having been born in Duckmanton. Importantly, however, we can now see that John declared his age at the time of this census to have been 30, which leads us to the registration record of his birth in the Mansfield district (which included Tibshelf) that was recorded in the June ¼ of 1879 under the single "T" spelling of his surname.

Turning our attention to his time in the army, John's 20528 service number indicates that he would have volunteered in the period 4th – 7th December 1914. When we consult the medal rolls, we discover that his overseas service began in France on 29th August 1915, and that all of his qualifying service was with the 12th Battalion of the Sherwood Foresters. All of this is not only entirely consistent with details quoted in his obituary, but would also indicate that, like Charles Banton, he was also a "founder member" of that battalion. As the details of this unit have already been disclosed under Charles's entry, they will not be repeated here.

Further details contained in "Soldiers Died…." inform us that John was killed in action at the age of 38 (when the 12th Battalion were in the Ypres Salient), and more information contained in his obituary tells us that he had in fact been hit by a shell splinter. At that time, the 24th Division had just played a role in the Battle of Messines, which had commenced on 7th June. In the week before that attack, the German lines had been subjected to a hail of over 3 ½ million shells, though even that was overshadowed on the first day of the offensive proper by the explosion of 19 subterranean mines which actually changed the Belgian landscape forever. It is believed that these devices killed 10,000 Germans within the 20 seconds that it took for them to be detonated, and that being heard in Dublin, it was also responsible for creating the largest ever man-made noise.

Sadly, his remains were either never found or could not be identified, and John, therefore, receives his official commemoration on the Menin Gate Memorial to the missing at Ypres. Not remembered in his native Tibshelf, he receives his only commemorations in the Chesterfield district at Sutton-cum-Duckmanton and Sutton Scarsdale.

BOWMAN, W.

WILLIAM BOWMAN

The records of the Commonwealth War Graves Commission show that William was the *"Husband of Mrs. E. Hollis (formerly Bowman), of 32, Arkwright Town, Chesterfield."* and therefore immediately establish his place on the memorial via a connection to the parish.

William and his wife Emma (Smith) were both natives of Whittington and had their wedding recorded in the Chesterfield district during the June ¼ of 1903. A line in his obituary informatively states that he had been living in the parish of Sutton-cum-Duckmanton since around 1907, and also adds a little more detail about those pre-war years by informing us that he had served for a number of years as a Warden at Duckmanton Church.

By the time that the 1911 Census was conducted, the couple were living at 42, Arkwright Town along with their 3 children, William Henry, 8, Hannah, 5, and Joseph, 1. At that date, William's occupation was listed as *"Coal Miner, Hewer"*, and further additional information from his obituary confirms that he had been employed at Markham No1 Colliery prior to his enlistment.

As neither his service nor pension records have survived, much of his time in the army sadly remains mysterious. We do know, however, from his 18494 service number that he is most likely to have volunteered with the Sherwood Foresters on either the 3rd or 4th November 1914, and from his entry in "Soldiers Died…." we also know that this took place in Chesterfield. As many of the men named on the memorial enlisted in the town, it should be documented that, in most cases, we know exactly where this would have taken place. When the members of the local Territorial Force were mobilised at the very beginning of the war, their then empty

Drill Halls became recruiting centres. In Chesterfield, the building that had served "A" Company of the 6th Battalion of the Sherwood Foresters was situated just beyond Saltergate, on Ashgate Road. Despite not being opened until September 1898 by Lord Roberts of Kandahar, it was originally known as the Diamond Jubilee Drill Hall. The building there, however, before being demolished, became better known to the townsfolk in later years as the Goldwell Rooms.

We know from the medal rolls that William's first overseas service was with the 11th Battalion of the regiment, and that he did not travel to France with them when they were first deployed. Though they landed at Boulogne on 25th August 1915, he did not join them until after 31st December, implying that for some reason he had been held back. There are several reasons why this might have been the case, with the more usual explanations being either sickness or injury. Fortunately, his obituary provides us with an extra clue, implying that he had first arrived overseas during either late January or early February 1916, which sadly means that he narrowly failed to meet the requirements for the award of the 1914-15 Star. Because of the lag in the timing between his enlistment and deployment as part of a reinforcement draft to 11th Battalion, and the additional absence of his service records, we are unfortunately unable to determine where or with which unit he had received his basic training.

As part of the 70th Brigade within the 23rd Division, we know that the 11th (Service) Battalion of the Sherwood Foresters were being taken out of the front line at about the time that William arrived. Much of his early foreign service would therefore have been undertaken in the vicinity of Bruay in Northern France. Calling on the crucial source of his obituary, we find that William had in fact been wounded three times before he was killed in action on 30th July 1917. It seems likely, therefore, that an injury sustained on one of those previous occasions had been serious enough to take him away from his unit, resulting in him being redirected to join the 17th Battalion of the regiment after he had recovered. He has, however, not been found on any of the casualty lists that were published in the newspapers, and so we have no clues about the timing of this transfer.

The 17th (Service) Battalion of the Sherwood Foresters had the subsidiary title of the "Welbeck Rangers", and had originally been raised in Nottingham on 1st June 1915 by the city's Mayor and a recruiting committee. They fought in a completely different organisation to William's old unit, being part of the 117th Brigade of the 39th Division. Having no knowledge of when he joined them, it is only pertinent to look at what they were doing at the time of his death. We do, however, know that William had been on home leave at the end of June 1917, and that this was in fact the only occasion on which he would ever have seen his youngest child. This was a son named James V. Bowman, whose birth was recorded in Chesterfield during the September ¼ of 1916.

At this point, we should perhaps begin to question the date given for his death, although all sources are adamant that it was 30th July. The War Diary of the battalion, however, is equally adamant that the unit only moved to take up its starting positions on that date in readiness for the following day, which was the first day of the Third Battle of Ypres. This document quite clearly (and perhaps even proudly) states that no casualties occurred whilst they were assembling. Their attack in the vicinity of Pilkem Ridge, however, was not launched until very early on the following day at 03:50 hrs. Whilst the entry in the diary for 1st August begins by saying that *"Yesterday we carried all before us, it was one of the Battalion's greatest days since its formation…"* there can, however, be little doubt that 41-year-old William did not live to see the sun set on it. His remains were never identified, and he therefore receives his official commemoration on the Menin Gate Memorial in Ypres.

Unlike the majority of the men commemorated at Sutton-cum-Duckmanton, it would appear that William is also remembered on several other memorials in the Chesterfield district. These include the Old Whittington Memorial, the Whittington Brushes Memorial, and the memorial inside St Bartholomew's Church in Old Whittington, all of which are located in the parish of his birth.

WORTH, H.

HERBERT WORTH

 The process followed to find Herbert's identity rather unconventionally began with his obituary. This supplied the information that he had been a married man whose wife had been living at 71, Arkwright Town at the time of his death. Unfortunately, it did not give her Christian name, but by finding his entry in the Army Registers of Soldiers' Effects this was discovered to have been Harriet. By next searching the registration data, it was possible to make the joint discovery that their wedding had been recorded in the Chesterfield district during the March ¼ of 1914, and that her maiden name had been Newbold. She was in fact the sister of the Thomas Newbold who is also commemorated on the memorial. Further interrogation of the registration database also found that the couple had a son named Lionel whose birth was recorded in the September ¼ of 1917.

The entry for Herbert in "Soldiers Died…." supplied the additional information that he had been born in Towcester, Northamptonshire, which then led to the discovery that the registration of this event had been made in that district during the March ¼ of 1894.

His entry in the 1911 Census shows him as a 17-year-old General Labourer, who was at that date still living with his parents (Walter and Maria) in Towcester, and which also informs us that his father was earning his living as a Farm Herdsman. Unfortunately, this does still leave some gaps in our knowledge of Herbert, and though we do not know exactly when he moved to Derbyshire, it is likely to have been circa 1912. His obituary does, however, provide additional information about his employment, by stating that he had been working at Bonds Main Colliery prior to his enlistment.

We are fortunate that he has a surviving service record, which shows us that Herbert actually enlisted into the Sherwood Foresters at Chesterfield on 26th August 1914, around 3 weeks after war had been declared. Numbered by them as 13887, his basic training was completed with their 4th (Extra Reserve) Battalion at Sunderland who, in addition to being a depot establishment for the regiment, also served on defensive duties as part of the Tyne Garrison. His overseas service commenced when he landed in France on 16th March 1915 and subsequently joined the Regiment's 1st Battalion as part of a sorely needed reinforcement draft, arriving just after they had played a major role in the Battle of Neuve Chapelle. He actually joined them in billets on the 19th March at Pont Du Hem with a party that included 2 officers and a further 115 enlisted men.

Herbert was, however, seriously injured just a few days later on 9th May, with a corresponding entry on his record stating *"gun shot wound to head."* The battalion were at that time supporting a unit of the East Lancashire in an attack at Rouges Bancs as a part of an operation designed to divert the attention of the Germans away from another attack that was being made by Britain's French allies further to the South. This action would enter the history books as the Battle of Aubers Ridge where, before they were withdrawn, the battalion suffered casualties in killed, wounded and missing totalling 359 men of all ranks. This, perhaps, needs some additional explanation as his obituary gives a false impression that his wound was sustained at the Battle of Neuve Chapelle. As we have seen, Herbert was not even in France when that battle was fought, though Aubers Ridge is actually situated on the Northern edge of that older battlefield. More helpfully, the obituary provides the detail that his injury was caused by a shell splinter, and this is probably more accurate than the information given on his service record. This document uses the term "gun shot wound" which, although sounding quite specific, was frequently used to describe a whole host of injuries that had been caused by any type of flying metal.

As a consequence of this injury, Herbert was shipped back to Britain within a few days to receive medical treatment and take the first footsteps on a long road to recovery. When he did return to France on 18th March 1916, it would be as a member of the Machine Gun Corps and, as his service record clearly gives the date of his transfer to them as 1st January 1916, he would therefore have been renumbered as 26718 on that date and have received his specialist training at Grantham. It is interesting to note that the Commonwealth War Graves Commission incorrectly gives his unit as the 5th Company, despite his service record making repeated mention that he had actually served with the 57th Company. This particular unit had originally been formed at Grantham but had moved to France and joined the 19th (Western) Division about a month before Herbert landed. This, therefore, makes him an early replacement rather than a "founder member" of the Company. As general details about the Machine Gun Corps have already been given under the entry for George Coe, they will not be repeated here.

According to his obituary, Herbert would be wounded twice more before he received the injury that would take his life, at the age of 23. In addition to this, his record also shows us that he had endured several bouts of sickness that required medical attention. He had, however, only been returned to France for 9 days after being on leave in the UK when he received the wound that would prove to be fatal. On the 3rd October 1917, the date on which he was both injured and lost the struggle for life, the 57th Company of the Machine Gun Corps were engaged in the last day of the Battle of Polygon Wood. This was an action fought as part of the epic Third Battle of Ypres which has perhaps entered the British psyche under the more familiar name of Passchendaele.

He receives his official commemoration at Larch Wood (Railway Cutting) Cemetery near Ypres. In addition to being remembered at Sutton-cum-Duckmanton and Sutton Scarsdale, his name also appears on the village memorial at Calow where his unit is inaccurately listed as having been the Sherwood Foresters.

WARDLE, A.

ALBERT HENRY WARDLE

Having outlined much of Albert's family background under the entry for his brother, James Edward Wardle, those details will not be repeated here.

With regard to Albert's time in the army, we are more fortunate than we were in the case of his younger brother, because his service record has survived. This shows us that he enlisted on new "Short Service" terms at Mansfield on 26th August 1914. It is interesting to note that his 6213 service number actually comes from the series issued by the Special Reserve, and together with his date of enlistment demonstrates that, despite his ultimately serving in the same battalion, the two brothers had not joined the army together. Further details from his service record indicate that he was originally posted to the Depot before being transferred to the 10th Battalion on 7th September. On joining, Albert listed his profession as *"Coal Miner"* and age as 26 years and 307 days, and from his obituary comes the added detail that he had originally been employed at Markham No 1 before moving to the Creswell Collieries.

Just as with his brother, his overseas service began on 14th July 1915 when the whole of the 10th Battalion landed at Boulogne, Albert was therefore undoubtedly also a "founder member" of the unit. Just like their predecessors in the 9th Battalion, they were originally raised in Derby with the bulk of their recruits largely coming from the same areas of the Nottinghamshire and Derbyshire coalfields. Neither of these two county towns ever raised a "Pals" battalion as such, though the ranks of the 9th and 10th battalions of the Sherwood Foresters were filled with knots of men from the same pit villages of both counties. Many of them had grown up together, been educated in the same village schools, had attended the same churches, played for the same Football or Cricket teams, worked in the same foundries or collieries, and would ultimately die together on the same fields of battle.

Amongst the details to be found in Albert's service record, there is evidence that he was wounded on 25th September 1915, and though this was the first day of the Battle of Loos, his battalion was on a different sector of the front on that date, close to the Belgian city of Ypres. Despite actually being at Sanctuary Wood near Hooge, they still, however, had an important role to play by creating a diversion to the main events that were taking place several miles to the South East. At 04:20 hours the men of the 10th battalion opened fire on the Germans in the trenches opposite, and were soon suffering under a hail of small arms and artillery fire that was sent back in retaliation. Hit by one of these German bullets, Albert was soon on his way back through the casualty clearing system and was returned to England for medical attention. It took him quite a while to recover, and it was not until the following year that he returned to France and rejoined the battalion on 4th February 1916, just before they were deployed to "The Bluff." His obituary casts more light on this injury by stating that *"a bullet entered his head behind the ear, passed down his neck, and lodged in his chest."* Strangely, however, it describes him as having received this wound at Mons, which is actually impossible as Albert had still been a civilian when that battle had been fought on 23rd August 1914.

Though Albert survived the events of 14th February, when the Germans drove the 10th Battalion out of their key position at The Bluff, he soon afterwards began receiving medical attention for an illness that recurred several times during the latter half of that year. He does, however, seem to have made a complete recovery by the beginning of 1917.

There is some discrepancy in the surviving evidence concerning the date that Albert's life had been lost, as whilst the official sources give this as the 13th October 1917, his obituary contains evidence which suggests that it occurred on the previous day. Where he lost his life is much easier to determine, because the 12th October marked the opening day of the First Battle of Passchendaele in the Ypres Salient. This perhaps requires a little clarification as this particular battle was a part of a much larger and longer lasting series of engagements which are more correctly known as the Third Battle of Ypres. The whole of this much larger offensive is however known to many simply as "Passchendaele." The engagement in which Albert lost his life was actually centred much more specifically around the Belgian village of that name.

Turning to their war diary for a more detailed version of events, we are shown that the battalion took part in an attack which started at 05:45 hrs on the 12th, and that an hour later they had achieved their first objective without encountering any opposition. After a short period of time spent consolidating this position, they moved on to their second and final objective and had successfully taken that by 07:30 hrs. The battalion stayed here overnight and repulsed a minor German counter-attack before being relieved on the night of the 13th/14th. Given the testimony of his officer, it would actually seem most likely that Albert lost his life during the second phase of the attack on the 12th. The Battalion War Diary confirms that the number of their casualties for those 2 days was approximately 17 killed and 154 wounded.

The news of 28-year-old Albert's death was conveyed to his parents in a letter written by Lieutenant C. F. S. Cox who stated that Albert had....

"died the noblest death of all, that of a British soldier on the battlefield. In action he was always a splendid example of bravery and determination to his fellow comrades, and we the officers and men miss his presence in the Company very much."

He went on to add that....

"It was the morning of the 12th of this month that he met his death, which was instantaneous. He had no suffering at all."

As with his brother, Albert's body was never identified, and he therefore receives his official commemoration on the Tyne Cot Memorial to the missing. Not far from where he fell, this memorial is located in the largest of the cemeteries of the Commonwealth War Graves Commission, containing the graves of almost 12,000 men from Britain and her Empire. His only commemorations in the Chesterfield district are on the memorials at Sutton-cum-Duckmanton and Sutton Scarsdale.

HARRIS, F.

FREDERICK ALFRED HARRIS

The connections between Frederick and the parish were easily established from a detailed description found in the files of the Commonwealth War Graves Commission. Their records not only give us his age at death, but supply the information that he was the *"Son of Henry and Susan Jane Harris, of Arkwright Town, Chesterfield, Derbyshire; husband of Sarah Ann Harris, of Arkwright Town, Chesterfield, Derbyshire."*

Checking his entry in "Soldiers Died...." however, reveals that his origins were not local, by showing that he had actually been born in the railway town of Swindon. It is by using this information to discover his birth registration record, made in the district of Highworth during the March ¼ of 1880, that enabled us to find his second Christian name.

The 1911 Census adds significantly more to our knowledge by showing that his father Henry had already passed away by that date, and that his widowed mother was then living with Frederick and his wife Sarah at 25, Arkwright Town. It also tells us that Frederick was working as a *"Colliery (Stone Miner)"*, whilst a line in his obituary confirms that he had actually been employed at Markham No1 Colliery. This census also introduces us to their daughter Lily, and from other sources we are also able to discover that she had been followed by a son named Frederick J. who had arrived later in that same year.

Checking the registration records for details of Frederick's own marriage leads us to discover that this was recorded in the Chesterfield district during the March ¼ of 1908. It also confirms that his wife Sarah, a native of Bolsover, had the maiden name of Steele.

Turning to his military service, a line in Frederick's obituary informs us that he had volunteered in November of 1914, and by using his 18372 service number we know that this is most likely to have taken place in Chesterfield either on or around the 2nd day of that month. The Medal Rolls show us that all of Frederick's overseas service was with the 11th (Service) Battalion of the Sherwood Foresters, and that he first landed in France on 27th August 1915. Unfortunately, we have neither service nor pension papers to confirm it, but it seems likely that he was a "founder member" of this battalion, because they first landed as a formed body at Boulogne on that same date. Originally formed at Derby in September of 1914 as a part of Lord Kitchener's 3rd "New Army", they were a battalion of the 70th Brigade within the 23rd Division.

Fredrick's obituary also informs us that he saw a great deal of action with this battalion, all of which he had survived *"without a scratch."* This was actually quite an accomplishment, because the Division took part in six major battles of the 1916 Somme offensive before going on to be involved in further engagements at the Battle of Messines and four more battles during the following year that each formed separate and distinct parts of Third Battle of Ypres (Passchendaele).

After all this fighting on the Western Front, the entire 23rd Division were re-deployed to Italy in November of 1917 and, after initially concentrating between Mantua and Marcaria, were involved in the fighting at the Asiago Plateau in June 1918. It is a tragic irony that Frederick, after being exposed to all this danger, would ultimately succumb to Pneumonia at the 24th Casualty Clearing Station on 14th July 1918 at the age of 38. The sad news being conveyed to his wife Sarah in a letter written by a Sister-in-Charge at that medical facility.

Frederick's final resting place is at Montecchio Precalcino Communal Cemetery Extension, in the Italian province of Vicenza. His only commemorations in the Chesterfield district are at Sutton-cum-Duckmanton and Sutton Scarsdale.

SMITH, E.

ERNEST SMITH

Usually, the prospect of discovering the identity of a casualty from a single source that lists him as "E. Smith" would be extremely daunting. We are, however, most fortunate in the case of Ernest, because the records of the Commonwealth War Graves Commission provide us with the supplementary information that he was the *"Husband of Eleanor Bryant (formerly Smith), of 129, Arkwright Town, Chesterfield, Derbyshire."* Immediately, therefore, we have both established his connection to the parish and been given access to his service number and unit details. To facilitate the equally challenging process of researching his family history, this same source also provides us with the information that he had been 30 years old when his life had been lost. Turning to his entry in "Soldiers Died....", we also find the additional details that he had been born in Sheffield and had enlisted in Chesterfield.

We are also fortunate that there is only one marriage record in the Chesterfield district between 1904 and 1919 in which an Ernest Smith had a bride named Eleanor. This was recorded in the September ¼ of 1910, and shows her maiden surname to have been Richmond. Their entry on the 1911 Census corroborates this by showing that the couple had then been married for one year, and also confirms the Arkwright Town address details that have already been established. In addition, this census also confirms other details found in the registration data, by showing that they had an infant daughter named Doris whose birth had been recorded in Chesterfield during the March ¼ of 1911. The couple would later go on to have a second daughter named Nellie who had her birth recorded in the same district during the September ¼ of 1913. She was in fact destined to be their only surviving child, as Doris sadly passed away in the early months of 1912. The 1911 Census also shows us that Ernest was then working as a *"Coal Miner Hewer"*, whilst added information from his obituary informs us that he was employed by the Staveley Coal and Iron Company at their Markham No2 Colliery.

With regard to his time in the army, his obituary states that he had enlisted in November 1914, and that certainly could be consistent with his 70677 service number. The numbers in that series are difficult to interpret, because they seem to have covered a variety of different types of attestation. We are, however, given an additional clue from his obituary which demonstrates that Ernest is likely to have enlisted in one of the battalions of the Territorial Force. The Sherwood Foresters initially had 4 Territorial battalions that were numbered as the 5th, 6th, 7th and 8th. Each of these, however, was split shortly after war was declared to form additional "2nd line" battalions numbered as the 2nd/5th, 2nd/6th, 2nd/7th, and 2nd/8th respectively. Of these, and despite no evidence having survived to support it, Ernest's initial service is most likely to have been with the $2^{nd}/6^{th}$, which had local connections.

Although he enlisted with the Territorial Force, Ernest most likely did not make the additional voluntary commitment to serve overseas, with the evidence for this coming from details given in his obituary stating that he had actually been sent to Ireland to play a role in quelling the Easter Rising of 1916. This same source also confirms that he had served there for several months before going to France, and this is further confirmed by his Medal Index Card which shows that he had not arrived in mainland Europe until after 31st December 1915. With service in Ireland classified as "Home Service", it was not officially recognised as being a "Theatre of War", and whilst those men who had not volunteered for overseas service could not be sent to France until after the introduction of the Military Service Act of 1916, they both could be and were sent to Ireland. The British government did not award any of the usual campaign medals for the Great War to any men for their service in Ireland, and no new campaign medals for those who fought in the rebellion were ever sanctioned. It was only in the second half of the 20th Century that clasps were authorised for the General Service Medal to recognise the service of those who had served in Northern Ireland during the more recent "troubles".

The Medal Rolls show us that Ernest initially served in France with the Regular Army 2nd Battalion of the regiment before later being transferred to the 15th (Service) Battalion in which he would be killed. From the records of the Commonwealth War Graves Commission, we do, however, have the extra piece of information that Ernest was serving with their "A" Company at the time of his death. A brief statement in his obituary also tells us that he was so severely wounded at some point that he spent six months in Bollington Hospital (a wartime military hospital, not far from Macclesfield in Cheshire). Sadly, no other information has been found on this, and we therefore do not know which battalion he was serving with at the time, anything about the nature of his injuries, or when they had been received.

The 15th (Service) Battalion of the regiment was first raised at Nottingham during February 1915 by the city's Mayor and a recruiting committee, and actually began its life as a "Bantam" unit. These specific types of unit were brought into being to allow men to volunteer who would otherwise have been rejected by the military because they had not attained the minimum regulation height. As the war ground on, however, it soon became apparent that it was impracticable to sort men by size, because the supply of additional shorter recruits proved inadequate for the task of providing sufficient numbers of reinforcements for them. The 15th Battalion of the Foresters were a unit of the 105th Brigade within the 35th Division, and had originally landed in France on 1st February 1916.

Reluctantly, the only alternative we have is to turn to the activities of this unit at the time of his death. The Battalion War Diary is, unfortunately, very sketchy about their activity at the time that Ernest was killed. Whilst it states that they were manning the front line trenches near Kemmel between the 13th - 17th July, and reports that they suffered 36 casualties during this period, it does not even attempt to break that down into dead and wounded, let alone provide us with their names. Ernest must, however, have been one of that number, as he was reported to have been killed in action on 14th July, with a letter from one of his officers describing his death as instantaneous. He receives his official commemoration at Abeele Aerodrome Military Cemetery near Ypres where his remains were interred, and is only remembered in the Chesterfield district at Sutton-cum-Duckmanton and Sutton Scarsdale.

GLOVER, J.

JOHN WILLIAM GLOVER

An obituary printed in the Derbyshire Times on 9th November 1918, just 2 days before the Armistice, positively identifies the memorial inscriptions for this man as referring to Driver John W. Glover of the Royal Field Artillery. It additionally informs us that his parents were living at 42, Arkwright Town when the news of his death was received, and therefore also makes this identification certain by connecting him with the parish.

Fortunately, the records of the Commonwealth War Graves Commission supply the Christian names of his parents as Charles and Mary, making it relatively easy to locate the family on the 1911 Census, and this document actually tells us a great deal. In addition to showing John as a 14-year-old Errand Boy, it also informs us that his father was a Coal Miner, and that they were then living on Cotterhill Lane in Brimington. Whilst it also shows that John was their eldest child (and informs us that he had actually been born at Middle Handley), the ages and places of birth of his siblings show that the family had first moved to New Whittington circa 1899 before taking up residence in Brimington circa 1906.

John's Birth was recorded in the Chesterfield registration district during the December ¼ of 1896, and his obituary confirms that his birthday was on the 10th October. The same registration data, however, also tells us that his parents Charles and Mary (Windle) had married in the Worksop registration district.

With neither service nor pension records having survived, we are reliant on several pieces of fragmentary information from various other sources to establish details of his time in the army. His obituary, however, informs us that he had been working at

Markham No1 Colliery prior to his enlistment, whilst his entry in "Soldiers Died...." confirms that he had volunteered in Chesterfield. Unfortunately, establishing when he joined the army is not easy, though evidence from men with similar service numbers does exist to suggest that this is most likely to have taken place during January 1915.

For information regarding his unit we were initially reliant upon the records of the Commonwealth War Graves Commission, which inform us that John died whilst serving with "B" Battery of the 246th (CCXLVI) Brigade of the Royal Field Artillery. This was a first line unit of the Territorial Force that served in the 49th (West Riding) Division, but which had been known as the 6th Battery of the II West Riding Brigade until May 1916. There is no doubt that John was not an original member of this unit, as they were deployed to France in mid-April 1915. Whilst his obituary states that he was drafted to France in August 1915, this gives us a false impression, as he was doubtless made aware that he was going on overseas service towards the end of that month, but would then have been allowed to take pre-embarkation leave. His Medal Index Card is quite clear in precisely dating his entry into France as having not actually occurred until 10th September.

It is also interesting to note that John's 83736 service number indicates that he was a regular army enlistment, and it is therefore almost certain that his initial service in France was with a different battery and brigade to the one in which he was serving at the time of his death. Not knowing either the identity of this other unit, nor being able to date his transfer, means that we cannot be certain about any of the details of his service up to the time that his life was lost. This does, however, give us a brief opportunity to provide some information about the Royal Artillery during the Great War era.

Despite being divided into Horse, Field and Garrison units, each of which had specialist functions, the men of the Royal Artillery of the Regular Army all wore the same cap badge. It would, however, be true to say that as the conflict evolved, the lighter guns of the Horse Artillery were seen to be less effective than those of the other two branches of the service, and were gradually phased out. Therefore, many of their units replaced their smaller calibre weapons with the ubiquitous and more versatile 18 pounder gun that was the mainstay of the Field Artillery units throughout the conflict. John's 246th Brigade, though never a unit of the Horse Artillery, had actually switched from 16 to 18 pounder guns during October 1915. By contrast, the Garrison Artillery units were responsible for the larger calibre, heavier and much less mobile siege guns.

Whilst it might be tempting to assume that the guns of the Field Artillery relied on a different means of transportation to their comrades in the "Horse" branch of the service, this was actually not the case. Their guns were also towed by teams of 6 horses which required Drivers to be mounted on the left hand horse of each of the 3 pairs. It would therefore be no exaggeration to say that John's experience of the war would have had much in common with the cavalrymen of a bygone age, and that he would have been both an experienced and accomplished equestrian.

Engaged in operations leading up to the crossing of the river Selle, the War Diary for John's unit records that 11 casualties were sustained on the 11th October, and it therefore seems likely that he was numbered amongst them. On that date, his battery was just to the South of Avesnes, indicating that he would have been moved through the casualty evacuation system to No 2 Casualty Clearing Station in the vicinity of Queant. John's obituary informs us that he died from wounds on the 15th October 1918, and his final resting place is in a dedicated Commonwealth War Graves cemetery, which forms an extension of the civilian graveyard serving the Commune of Queant in the Pas de Calais. This settlement lies roughly in the centre of a triangle that may be drawn by connecting the larger urban areas of Arras, Cambrai and Bapaume. His only commemorations in the Chesterfield district are at Sutton-cum-Duckmanton and Sutton Scarsdale.

LONGDEN, A.

ALBERT LONGDEN

 The obituary published for Albert in the 19th November 1918 edition of the Derbyshire Times provided us with very little information. It does, however, confirm that the news of his death was received by his mother in Duckmanton, and therefore immediately establishes a connection between the name on the memorial, the parish and this Driver of the Royal Field Artillery. The Commonwealth War Graves Commission has only one record for a casualty named as an "A. Longden" who served with the Royal Field Artillery, but whilst this confirms that his Christian name had been Albert, it sadly gives no details concerning either his home or family. It falls to the Army Registers of Soldiers' Effects to provide the vital information that Albert had been married, and that the Christian name of his widow was Agnes.

The record for this man in "Soldiers Died...." added to the details that we had already established by both showing that he had enlisted in Mansfield, and describing him as being a resident of Bolsover. Mysteriously, whilst a check of the memorials in that place fails to find any mention of him, it has, however, been discovered that he is also remembered on the memorial at Calow.

The details of Albert's marriage are relatively easy to establish using the registration data. These records show that he married Agnes Simcoe in the Chesterfield registration district during the September ¼ of 1912. A slightly different interrogation of the same database goes on to reveal that the couple were soon blessed with their twins, Albert and Theresa, and that they then went on to have two more sons who both tragically had very short lives. They were

Herbert, who was born (and died) in 1914, and Walter who was born in 1916 and died in 1919.

It is only by consulting the census returns for 1901 and 1911 that we can discover any information about Albert's parents, who were William and Sarah. The earlier document of the two shows us that William was a Market Gardener on Inkersall Lane, though additional research revealed that he died in 1904. By the date of the 1911 Census, Albert was living with his widowed mother at an address given as Tom Lane End, Duckmanton, and was then working as an *"Underground Roadman"* in a local coal mine. His obituary corroborates this, and supplies the additional information that he had been employed at Markham No 1 Colliery prior to his enlistment. Having established Albert's age via the census returns, we were also finally able to discover that his birth had been recorded in the Chesterfield district during the March ¼ of 1887.

With no surviving service or pension documents having been traced for Albert, we have to look at other sources to determine more details about his time in the army. His L/7942 service number proves to be a useful starting point, because its "L" prefix indicates that he had been "locally recruited." This informs us that he not only enlisted voluntarily, but that he almost certainly did so on the wartime introduced terms of "3 years or the duration." This is also conveniently supported by evidence from his obituary which informs us that he had actually received his basic training in Nottingham. Sadly, there is no further information contained in this source that can give us any clue about the date of his enlistment, but using the date of his death and the amount paid for his gratuity indicates that Albert joined the army in either late January or early February 1915. We are, however, more fortunate with determining when he first served overseas, as his obituary informs us that he was first sent to France in January 1916. Additionally, his lack of entitlement to a 1914-15 Star would also support that his overseas service could not have begun before 31st December 1915.

It is also interesting to note that the "D" designation of the battery that he was serving with indicates that Albert was involved with howitzers rather than the more common 18 pounder guns of the Royal Field Artillery. Although they were very similar weapons, the howitzers were designed to fire at higher trajectories, and were therefore able to target the enemy "indirectly" by firing over the tops of hills and other obstacles on the battlefield. These weapons also played a major role in cutting enemy wire with shrapnel shells, and their crews were also trained to participate in laying down impenetrable curtains of fire. Used to great effect, the combined firepower provided by several batteries working in unison could either be fixed or made to "creep" ahead of advancing infantry. These barrages could also be used to target the areas behind the enemy front lines, where these curtains of shellfire effectively sealed off their forward positions, simultaneously making it impossible for an enemy to retreat and preventing them from being either re-supplied or reinforced.

The 153rd (CLIII) Brigade with which Albert was serving at the time of his death underwent some organisational change during the course of the war. His "D" battery, for example, had originally been designated "C" Battery of the 154th (CLIV) Brigade. With his arrival in France pre-dating that change, it is therefore possible that his early service could have been with that older formation. Without surviving service papers, however, we cannot be certain that this was the case, particularly as their arrival in France took place during November 1915, thereby indicating that Albert could either have been part of a later reinforcement draft for them, or may just as easily have begun his overseas service with a different and unknown unit.

As a formation of the 36th (Ulster) Division, we are, however, able to determine that on the day that Albert was killed, 27th October 1918, his battery would have been engaged in the Action at Ooteghem. Fought in Belgium as part of the Allied "Advance to Victory", this particular battlefield lies very close to where Albert was laid to rest at the age of 31. Though originally interred at Desselghem Churchyard, his remains were removed after the war and reburied at Harlebeke New British Cemetery in West Flanders. He therefore now lies alongside over 900 other British troops who receive their official commemorations in that place, and who also lost their lives in the Great War.

HOBSON, W.

WILLIAM ALFRED HOBSON

The records of the Commonwealth War Graves Commission confirm the identification of this man by stating that he was the *"Son of Joseph and Mary Hobson, of 19, East Terrace, Milford, nr. Derby; husband of Ellen Hobson, of 94, Arkwright Town, nr. Chesterfield."* They also reveal him to have been a tragic casualty who actually lost his life on 13th November 1918, two days after the Armistice had come into effect.

The 1911 Census shows us that there were two Hobson households in Arkwright at that date. William was living with his wife Ellen and their young family at No 26, whilst the slightly older Harry Hobson and his wife Mary Elizabeth were with their family at No 16. Further evidence from the 1891 Census shows that they were in fact brothers, and part of a large family from Milford near Belper. Their father Joseph was a Stoker at a cotton bleach works at that date, but by 1911 both sons were working as Miners in the local pits, and we know from his obituary that William was employed at Markham No1 Colliery. We are also told by this same newspaper coverage that his wife Ellen was actually living at 41, Carr Vale Cottages at the time of his death.

No registration data for the marriage of William and Ellen has been found, but parish records show that they were married at Milford on 2nd July 1904 and additionally reveal that her maiden name had been Watson. The 1911 Census shows that their first child, William Albert, was born at Belper circa 1906, whilst their daughter Hilda Mary had her birth registered in the Chesterfield district during the September ¼ of 1909. We can, therefore, theorise that their association with Arkwright began somewhere between those two dates. William's obituary informs us that he left a widow and 5 children, and registration data from the Chesterfield district shows the other three to have been Rose, E., Joseph, and Alfred, who all had their births registered in Chesterfield during 1912, 1915, and 1918 respectively.

From his 18444 service number we can calculate that William almost certainly enlisted on 3rd November 1914, and whilst he has no entry in "Soldiers Died...." to confirm it, this probably happened in Chesterfield. His initial training in the UK is most likely to have been with either of the 3rd or 4th Battalions of the Sherwood Foresters, but unfortunately, we are unable to narrow that down any further. When it comes to his overseas service, however, his entries on the Medal Rolls show that he moved 4 times between the 2nd and 10th Battalions of the regiment. However, we can be fairly confident that his active service began with the 2nd Battalion after he landed in France for the first time on 21st April 1915.

There is one interesting clue in his obituary about this alternating service between battalions, because it states that he was *"returned to civil life after 2 ½ years with the colours"*, indicating that he came back to England in May 1917. It goes on to say that he was *"ordered to rejoin the regiment on April 9th {1918} and about a fortnight later was sent to France."* However, we are neither told which battalion he left in 1917 or which one he had joined on his return to active service a year later. Similarly, we are not given any clues about why he had returned to England. William has not been found on any casualty lists that were published in the press between when he first landed in France and his death, and with no surviving service papers, the reasons behind this are likely to remain a mystery.

The background to the decision that was taken for him to return to active service in 1918 is, however, much easier to fathom. William's recall to the Colours was doubtless made in response to what is seen by many to have been the greatest crisis of the war, when the Germans unleashed an offensive with the objective of gaining a rapid victory before any intervention by the USA could prevent it. Launched on 21st March 1918, and bolstered by 50 Divisions of extra troops that had been released after the collapse of resistance on the Russian Front the previous year, the German advance initially seemed to be unstoppable.

The obituary that was printed for William in the Derbyshire Times does make it clear that he died from wounds, and was not a victim of the 1918 Spanish Flu pandemic that swept across Europe claiming millions of lives during that final year of the war. We also know that he was serving with the 10th Battalion at that time, and can therefore turn our attention to their Battalion War Diary in those closing days of the hostilities. The last date on which any casualties were recorded was the 4th November, when they had taken part in a successful attack to the West of Cambrai near Poix-Du-Nord and the Foret de Mormal.

Evacuated through the casualty clearing system, William was ultimately admitted to No16 General Hospital. Located close to the coastal town of Le Treport, this is where, at the age of 37, he died. He receives his official commemoration close to that town at Mont Huon Military Cemetery, where his remains were interred. His only commemorations in the Chesterfield district are at Sutton-cum-Duckmanton and Sutton Scarsdale.

CURREY, J.

JOHN THOMAS CURREY

We are most unfortunate in the case of John that, whilst the obituary that appeared for him in the edition of the Derbyshire Times that was published on 11th January 1919 has survived, it is so badly faded that it cannot now be read. All that could be salvaged from what seems to have been that quite extensive coverage was his portrait. In fact, we are doubly unfortunate because, as his death occurred after the Armistice, he also receives no entry in "Soldiers Died...."

We were therefore reliant on other sources to begin our investigations into John's story. The Records of the Commonwealth War Graves Commission provided a useful starting point by informing us that his life had been lost on 30th December 1918 whilst he was serving as a Private of the Sherwood Foresters with a service number of 120516. They also tell us that he was 27 years of age and that he had been the husband of *"Annie Currey of Sutton-cum-Duckmanton."* Although it is not stated in their records, we were also able to tell, because he is buried in the churchyard at Duckmanton, that he must have died in the UK. When all these strands of evidence are viewed together they prove sufficient to establish the identity of this man beyond doubt.

Turning next to the 1911 Census, we find the record of a John Thomas Currey, aged 19, living with his parents Samuel and Emily at an address in Chesterfield. This document also usefully informs us that he had been born in "Greasbury" though this is actually thought to be a reference to Greasborough near Rotherham. Quite conclusively, he is actually the only John Currey to appear on the 1911 Census who was residing in Derbyshire at that date. Whilst his father lists his occupation at that time as being a Labourer at the

Staveley Coal and Iron Company, John was described as being a Coal Miner.

Going on to consult the registration data, we discover that only one marriage record matches the information that we already have for John. This shows that his wife's maiden name had been Taylor, and that the ceremony had been conducted in the Rotherham district during the December ¼ of 1915.

From a military viewpoint, we are much more fortunate than we were with his obituary, because his service record has survived. This source tells us that whilst he was conscripted on 24th June 1916, he was not actually mobilised to join the Sherwood Foresters at Derby until 15th July 1918. It also confirms that his wife was then living at 63, Arkwright Town, and adds further useful family information by showing that the couple had a son, Joseph Samuel, who had been born on 23rd December 1916.

After first joining the regiment at Derby, he was sent to undertake his basic training with the 3rd (Reserve) Battalion at Sunderland where they had been forming part of the Tyne Garrison since May 1915. After over 4 years of war, with all of its trials and tribulations, it doubtless came as a relief to both John and his family that the Armistice came into effect before it was deemed that he was ready to be sent overseas on active service. Their delight at this development was, however, destined to be tragically short-lived, because he became ill on the 24th November and was admitted to the Walkergate Fever Hospital in Newcastle. It was here that he died on 30th December, with the cause of his loss being attributed to Cerebro-Spinal Fever, a condition perhaps better known to us today as Meningococcal Meningitis.

His body would almost certainly have been sent back by rail for burial at Duckmanton, where his official commemoration therefore takes the form of his Commonwealth War Graves headstone. His only other commemorations anywhere within the Chesterfield district are on the memorials at Sutton-cum-Duckmanton and Sutton Scarsdale.

THE UNATTRIBUTABLE MEMORIAL INSCRIPTIONS FOR THE GREAT WAR

There are three inscriptions for casualties of the Great War named on the metal plate attached to the base of the memorial that we have been unable to identify, though one of these names is extremely likely to have been placed there in error. Each of these inscriptions, however, will be dealt with here in some detail.

ATTENBOROUGH, J.

Whilst the records of the Commonwealth War Graves Commission show that just 11 casualties of the Great War match this combination of surname and initial, we have been unable to identify the one that this inscription was intended to commemorate. The nearest possibilities geographically would seem to be two brothers from Hasland named John and Jabez. Unfortunately, no connection to the parish of Sutton-cum-Duckmanton has been established for either of them, though they are both commemorated on the memorial at Hasland. A third local possibility also exists in the form of another fatality named John. His records, however, contain family information that links him to Mansfield and again fail to make any connection with Sutton-cum-Duckmanton.

BARBER, C.

This inscription on the memorial is something of an enigma, as it did not appear in either the original list of names that were carved directly into the stonework of the plinth or on the tablet in St. Mary's Church at Sutton Scarsdale. Whilst the records of the Commonwealth War Graves Commission show 32 casualties which would fit this name, none of their records, which contain additional information, show that any of them had any connection with Derbyshire. In addition, in an era from which it has been possible to find obituaries in the local press for the overwhelming majority of the Great War Casualties, no entries have been located that match this combination of initial and surname. It can also be confirmed that there is no record of a C. Barber having lived in the parish when the 1891, 1901 or 1911 censuses were conducted.

It is thought likely that this inscription should actually have related to Charles Banton, whose name was included on both of the original memorials, but was initially missing from the engraved metal plate and subsequently added at a later date. It will be noted that both of the original memorials listed 27 names as having been casualties of the Great War, whilst the metal plate currently attached to it contains 28.

WILSON, E.

This name appeared on both of the original memorials, though the spelling of it was different on each. The carving on the base of the cross gives it as "E. WILLSON PTE", whilst the memorial tablet in St. Mary's Church lists him as "WILSON, E." Despite the Commonwealth War Graves Commission holding multiple records for men that would match this name, none of them have any obvious links to the parish. In addition, there is no entry for anyone of this name in the parish on the 1911 Census, no association for this name to anyone in our area in "Soldiers Died....", and no matching obituary is recorded as having appeared in the local press.

GREAT WAR CASUALTIES ASSOCIATED WITH THE DISTRICT THAT ARE NOT NAMED ON THE MEMORIAL

Although the following are not named on the memorial, evidence does exist which connects them to the immediate local area. There are many reasons why their names may not have been added originally, and it should be remembered that they may either have been excluded at the request of their next of kin or because they were deemed not to have qualified under the original terms that were drawn up for inclusion.

This is not intended to be a complete list of non-commemorations. These names and details merely surfaced during the course of investigations into those who are named on the memorial, and there may be several others who have yet to be discovered. At this distance in time from the related events, it would, in any case, be impossible to produce any list of non-commemorations that could be guaranteed as being complete.

Not falling under the terms of reference for the original project, these details are, however, given here in respectful acknowledgement of their sacrifice.

40189, Charles Edward Bowler, 1st Bn. Royal Dublin Fusiliers who fell 9th August 1917. Linked by information held by the Commonwealth War Graves Commission which states that he was the *"Son of William Charles and Emily Bowler, of Duckmanton, Chesterfield; husband of Clemmy Bowler, of 68A, Morley St., Bradford, Yorks."*

26110, Corporal Harry Evans, 5th Bn. King's Shropshire Light Infantry who fell 22nd August 1917. Harry is linked to the parish by his entry in "Soldiers Died…." which states that he was born in Duckmanton, Derbyshire.

19896, George Lowe, 9th Bn. Sherwood Foresters who fell 15th June 1918. George is linked to the parish by his entry in "Soldiers Died...." which states that he was born in Duckmanton, Derbyshire.

10795 or 107951, Henry Thompson Roberts, 6th Bn. York & Lancaster Regiment who fell 14th June 1917. Henry is linked to the parish by his entry in "Soldiers Died...." which states that he was born in Duckmanton, Derbyshire.

SECTION TWO

THE SECOND WORLD WAR
1939-45

A total of 19 names are listed on the memorial relating to casualties of the Second World War, though sadly, it has only been possible to discover the identities of 17 of the men that these inscriptions commemorate. On the monument itself, it is obvious that 16 of those named were originally listed in something close to alphabetical order whilst the other 3 are shown out of sequence, indicating that they are likely to have been added at some later date. Once again, this system of ordering has been ignored in the organisation of this work, and their biographies have instead been presented in the order in which their lives were lost.

It became apparent in the early stages of the research that, as with the recording of the names for the Great War, there are also issues with some of the spellings that are found on the memorial for these later casualties. For example, the inscription for "J. Crookes" has actually been identified as being intended to commemorate John Crook. The format for each individual story therefore remains unchanged from that used for the casualties of the Great War. Each heading is a verbatim representation of the spelling that appears on the memorial but ordered as surname followed by initial(s). The sub heading gives, where known, the full name of each casualty with any spelling errors corrected.

The casualties of the Second World War are actually much more difficult to verify than those of the Great War, simply because fewer primary sources for them are readily available. For example, there are no Medal Index Cards (because the medals issued to British service personnel for this conflict were not named), there is no equivalent of "Soldiers Died....", and neither service records, pension records, nor census returns later than that for 1911 have yet been released into the public domain. This means that we are much more reliant upon the records of the Commonwealth War

Graves Commission together with any obituaries that were published in the local press. With reference to the local newspapers, however, we are not only reduced to a single source, because the Derbyshire Courier ceased to exist in 1922, but have also found that far fewer obituaries were published than had been the case during the Great War era.

Fortunately, with the casualties of the Second World War being far fewer than those sustained during the Great War, the records of the Commonwealth War Graves Commission give fewer matching search results for many of the names that we needed to find. We are also fortunate that the records they hold for the casualties of the Second World War tend to be more complete, with a higher proportion of them providing at least some information about families, ages at death, and places of residence. The extra information gained from these records however does not make up for the lack of the other sources that we had been able to consult for the casualties of the Great War. Unfortunately, this same dearth of information also, therefore, means that fewer meaningful statistics can be compiled regarding these later casualties.

It is interesting to note that the casualties of the Second World War do actually tell us something about the development of the parish in the inter-war years. For example, it was noticed straight away that a much higher proportion of the casualties had their origins in the district, with over 76% of them having had their births registered in Chesterfield. It was also noted that ½ of the remainder had theirs recorded in adjacent districts rather than in the other more distant counties that we encountered when compiling data for those who fell in the Great War. It is also interesting to note that, in testament to where the expansion in house building had taken place in the parish during those inter-war years, a far higher proportion its casualties of the Second World War had associations with Duckmanton rather than Arkwright Town. Where their origins and/or places of residence are known, almost 53% connect to the former, whilst only 29% relate to the latter.

With universal conscription having been introduced on the same date that war was declared, it becomes meaningless to discuss recruitment for the Second World War in the same terms that we did for the Great War. In any case, with the lack of information available regarding the men's individual enlistment dates, any such analysis is impossible. From the limited information that has been found, there is evidence to show that only one of these men had joined the army before the outbreak of war, though there could perhaps have been others. It would, however, seem certain that the overwhelming majority of these men came into the armed services as conscripts after 3rd September 1939. We are also similarly less well informed about where these men had been employed before their military service. Where any evidence of their civilian occupations has been found, it does, however, point firmly to the continued dominance of the coal mining industry within the parish, and several of the obituaries that were printed for these men inform us that their subjects had worked at the Markham collieries.

Another major difference between the casualties of the Second World War and those of the Great War is immediately obvious. The Army in particular had learned the harsh lessons of the "Pals" battalions from that earlier era, which had seen entire districts plunged into mourning in the wake of the disastrous first day of the 1916 Somme offensive. We therefore see this reflected in an increased diversity of the units with which these local men had been serving when their lives were lost. The swathes of Sherwood Foresters that we encountered amongst the casualties of the Great War were simply not repeated. In fact, only one man named on the parish memorial for the Second World War had been serving with that regiment. The diversity that we see was also of course increased because of the increased importance of the flying services, whose casualties account for almost 18% of the men that we have been able to identify.

It is certainly interesting and perhaps surprising to note that, with regard to Sutton-cum-Duckmanton, the average age of her casualties in the Second World War was just 24, a full 4 years younger than that of the sons she had lost in the Great War. This is also reflected in the range of their ages, with the youngest at 18 and the eldest at 33. Perhaps as a result of losing their lives at these younger ages, fewer of them left widows and children behind, though there were still eight women who did not see their husbands return, and at least seven children that were left without fathers.

One small comfort, perhaps, is that the remains of the dead were much better accounted for in this conflict, and that only around 18% of the Second World War dead from the parish received their official commemorations on memorials to the missing. Another perhaps less startling feature of the Sutton-cum-Duckmanton casualties of this later conflict is that they lost their lives in a wide variety of different locations. Whilst 29% of them were lost in the North African campaign, a closer examination reveals that they actually died in three different countries within that region. The fact that others were lost in Crete, Burma, Italy, Sicily and Hong Kong demonstrates a huge diversity of service, though the more expected casualties are also present, who lost their lives in France, Belgium and Holland.

THE FALLEN
OF
THE SECOND WORLD WAR
1939 - 1945

Thomas Sims	27th May 1941
Kenneth Sims	4th August 1941
Victor Ernest Plumb	23rd November 1941
Dennis Walter Bland	9th April 1942
Harry Winnard	10th February 1943
Thomas Edmund Curry	22nd April 1943
Robert William Bryon	23rd April 1943
Roy Wright Madin	11th July 1943
Charles William Moore	24th August 1943
Charles Wharton	20th October 1943
Gordon Joseph William Peck	11th April 1944
John Penney	13th May 1944
Edward Glenn	7th June 1944
John Crook	27th June 1944
Baden Clarke	7th February 1945
Roy Marples	6th March 1945
Joseph Kirby Alvey	31st March 1945
R. T. Cooper	Unidentified
C. G. Daniel	Unidentified

BIOGRAPHIES
OF THOSE WHO FELL
IN THE SECOND WORLD WAR

SIMS, T.

THOMAS SIMS

The identification of this man was solely reliant upon the records of the Commonwealth War Graves Commission, as no obituary for Thomas has been traced. The information that they hold, however, is conclusive because it declares him to have been the *"Son of John and Harriett B. Sims, of Arkwright Town, Derbyshire."* In addition to this, it also supplies the tragic information that *"His brother Kenneth also died on service.",* and tells us that Thomas had been just 25 years old when his life was lost.

The registration data reveals that his father John had married Harriet Bannister Ramsdale in the Chesterfield district during the March ¼ of 1908, and also provides us with a birth record for Thomas that was made in the same district during the March ¼ of 1916. A little confusingly, the latter gives the maiden surname of his mother as Rawsdale, though other sources demonstrate this to be an error.

The information that the Commonwealth War Graves Commission holds concerning his service shows that Thomas, with the number 4857929, had been a Private with the 2nd Battalion of the Leicestershire Regiment at the time of his death. As a unit of the 16th Infantry Brigade, this battalion of the pre-war Regular Army was in Palestine in September of 1939, but moved to North Africa a year later and saw active service in the first major British campaign in the Western Desert at Sidi Barany during December. Following on from this, they were involved at the Battle of Bardia, and the advances through Buq Buq and Solhuh, which were all parts of Operation Compass that saw a heavy defeat inflicted on the Italians. April of 1941 saw them once again engaged in this theatre of war at Mersa Matruh, though this time their opponents were Erwin Rommel's newly arrived German Afrika Korps.

All this was set to change, however, when a new crisis loomed on the opposite side of the Mediterranean. After the German advance on mainland Greece had proved to be unstoppable, it was soon realised that the island of Crete was likely to become their next target, and the 2nd Leicesters were rushed there to bolster the existing garrison. This saw the battalion temporarily become a unit of the 14th infantry Brigade, which initially had responsibility for defending a key sector in the centre of the Northern coast of the island around Heraklion. The key strategic sites that they were sent to protect in this area were, however, not just restricted to its important port facilities, but also included a recently constructed airfield.

When the Germans launched their attack on the island on 20th May 1941 it almost certainly did not come as a complete surprise, though there is some evidence to suggest that their original assault was initially thought to have been a diversion. The manner in which it was actually delivered had, however, almost certainly not been anticipated. At around 08:00 hrs, the skies above Maleme and Chania were filled with German Junkers 52 transport planes, which heralded a mass deployment of airborne troops. Even as this initial force landed and launched their attack, they were swiftly assisted and reinforced by a second wave that began to arrive in gliders. Despite the speed and efficiency of their arrival and deployment, the defending Allied troops in that area were, however, still able to mount such a stout resistance that the Germans not only suffered heavy casualties but were initially held in check.

Unfortunately, this would not signal the end of the German invasion, for later in the day fresh waves of both paratroopers and glider borne troops began to land at Rethymno and Heraklion where Thomas' battalion was stationed. Once again, the defending troops in these locations initially proved to be more than a match for the Germans, inflicting heavy casualties on them and denying them their objectives. By the evening of the following day, however, the situation had worsened for the Allies, and despite the Axis forces suffering several more setbacks over succeeding days it was they who would eventually gain the upper hand. One of the key factors behind this reversal lay in the Germans having established air superiority, enabling them to bomb both the Allied land forces and the supporting ships of the Royal Navy with impunity.

We have no details regarding the exact circumstances of Thomas' death, but the records of the Leicestershire Regiment state that he was killed in action at Suda Bay on 27th May. Though the loss of Crete was a disaster, it was decidedly not a rout. The Allied forces engaged continued to put up a dogged resistance to the very last, and well over half of their number were successfully evacuated from the island before it fell into German hands on 1st June.

Thomas receives his official commemoration at Suda Bay War Cemetery. It should be noted, however, that his name actually appears on a special memorial there because his remains are thought to be amongst those of 776 casualties which could not be individually identified.

SIMS, K.

KENNETH SIMS

Just as with his older brother Thomas, the identification of Kenneth was once again solely reliant upon the records of the Commonwealth War Graves Commission, because similarly, we have no obituary for him. The information that they hold, however, is again conclusive, because it declares that he was the *"Son of John and Harriett B. Sims, of Arkwright Town, Derbyshire"*, before adding a similar note to the one found on his brother's record confirming that *"his brother Thomas also died on service."* This same source also gives Kenneth's age at death as having been just 23. The double tragedy endured by this family was fortunately unique in the parish during the Second World War, though the loss of two of their boys was doubtless made even more devastating as their deaths were separated by a mere 69 days.

Having already discussed the details of their parents under the section dedicated to his brother, the only additional genealogical information that needs to be added here is confirmation that Kenneth's birth was registered in the Chesterfield district during the September ¼ of 1918. No records have been found which indicate that he had ever been married.

Some details of Kenneth's military service can be found in the files of the Commonwealth War Graves Commission. Though brief, this record informs us that he had been serving as a Gunner with the Royal Artillery under the number 1502642 when his life was lost, and that he had been with the 16th Battery of their 2nd Heavy Anti-Aircraft Regiment. This battery, however, has a complex history, as it moved between different Heavy Anti-Aircraft Regiments during the course of the war. Originally it was part of the 4th such regiment, but then moved to the 1st before being transferred to the 2nd. It was also widely travelled, and saw service in a variety of different theatres.

The 2nd Heavy Anti-Aircraft Regiment, including Kenneth's 16th Battery, arrived in Suez on 1st September 1940, and it is perhaps reasonable to assume that Kenneth was with them by that date. Equipped with eight 3.7" guns, they moved West along the coast and took up positions at Marsa Matruh on 2nd October. By early the following month, however, they had been formed up for mobile operations. When the Regimental Headquarters moved to Cairo at the end of December, Kenneth's 16th Battery (which had remained at Marsa Matruh), then temporarily became a unit of the newly arrived 51st Heavy Anti-Aircraft Regiment. This arrangement, however, did not last, as the battery re-joined the headquarters in Greece during February of 1941 and served in the campaign there until moving to the island of Crete at the end of April. The battery had actually left its guns behind in Greece, and its stay in Crete was only destined to be very brief before it moved yet again. Landing in Alexandria on 2nd May, and still without its guns, the men of the 16th Battery were immediately deployed to the Delta where they served as infantry in an anti-parachute role.

Whilst we know that he died on 4th August 1941, the exact circumstances of Kenneth's death have unfortunately not been discovered. The records of the Commonwealth War Graves Commission do, however, inform us that most of the graves in the cemetery where he is buried belong to servicemen who had either died in the local hospitals or a nearby transit camp. His final resting place is at the Port Said War Memorial Cemetery, and therefore, of the two brothers, he lies the furthest away from home.

PLUM, V.

VICTOR ERNEST PLUMB

Determining the identification of the man behind this inscription on the memorial fortunately proved to be quite straightforward, despite an early setback in which it was discovered that the records of the Commonwealth War Graves Commission simply contained no entries for anyone named "V. Plum." Further searches of their database, however, revealed that they did have an entry for a "V. Plumb" that related to the Second World War. It was soon obvious that the memorial inscription was actually intended to commemorate this casualty, as the additional personal information that they hold for him states that he had been the *"Son of William Ernest and Gertrude Plumb, of Duckmanton, Derbyshire."*

Consulting the registration data, we discover a unique record which corresponds with a "Victor E. Plumb" who could have lost his life at the age of 22 in 1941. This document tells us that his birth was recorded in the Chesterfield district during the September ¼ of 1919, and also provides the useful additional information that the maiden name of his mother had been Merricks. This leads instantly to the discovery of a further unique record showing that the marriage of his parents had been recorded in the same district during the March ¼ of 1915.

As with so many of the local casualties from the Second World War, no obituary has been traced for Victor in the local press, though an enigmatic personal advert was placed in the Derbyshire Times which mentioned his name. Printed on the 7th May 1943, almost 18 months after his death, it reads as follows:

"Will the parents of Trooper Victor Plumb, M.E.F., of Duckmanton, please communicate with Trooper J. Silcock of 30, St. Augustines Mount, Chesterfield."

Sadly, we will perhaps never know if Victor's family were ever made aware of this advert, or if they ever responded to it. Similarly, we have been left with no clues regarding why Trooper Silcock obviously thought it was so important that they should contact him. These few lines, however, do have value by reinforcing his connection with the parish.

Numbered as 7906014, Victor was serving with the 4th County of London Yeomanry (Sharpshooters) at the time of his death on 23rd November 1941. Though their title perhaps hints at them being a long established regiment with a deep-rooted history, they were in fact a wartime raised unit. Their birth can actually be traced to the 27th September 1939 when, in line with plans to double the size of the existing Territorial Army, the formation of this unit began with a nucleus of men detached from the 3rd County of London Yeomanry (Sharpshooters). It should also be noted that, though styled as cavalry, they were actually an armoured unit from the very beginning, and were assigned to the 22nd Heavy Armoured Brigade.

Initially on Home Service, this Brigade originally became a part of the 2nd Armoured Division in January 1940 before being transferred into the 1st Armoured Division during October of that same year. Their deployment for overseas service did not actually begin until 15th August 1941, when the brigade embarked for Egypt. They were the first unit from their Division to land in that theatre of operations, and were attached to the 7th Armoured Division upon their arrival in November as part of the preparations for the forthcoming battles of Operation Crusader. This formation would, of course, become much more familiarly known as the "Desert Rats" of the 8th Army, and would later play a decisive role in defeating the Axis forces in North Africa. Sadly, Victor was destined to be one of their early casualties, and did not live to see any of those later battle honours added to the record of his regiment.

The objective of Operation Crusader was the lifting of the Siege of Tobruk, where a largely Australian garrison had been isolated since

10th April 1941 denying the Axis powers access to its strategically important port facilities. The troops trapped there were subjected to constant German attacks, and despite their having been several previous attempts to break the siege, they would not actually be relieved until 27th November. Relief operations began on 18th November when Victor's 22nd Armoured Brigade started their advance, and by the following morning they were heavily engaged near Bir el Gubi with the Italian Ariete Division. Victor's Brigade was also involved in another hotly contested battle on the 20th, before they were ordered to disengage and move East in support of 4th Armoured Brigade who had themselves been encountering stiff opposition from the German 15th Panzer Division.

On the 21st November, Victor's Brigade once again found themselves in another fierce engagement, this time in the vicinity of Sidi Rezegh, where the fighting continued into the following day. With the date of his death given as 23rd November, it is equally likely that Victor was either killed in action on that date or died of wounds received in any of the actions in which his Brigade had fought over the previous days. His final resting place is at Knightsbridge War Cemetery near Acroma in Libya.

BLAND, D. W.

DENNIS WALTER BLAND

The records of the Commonwealth War Graves Commission list six fallen of the Second World War who could have been described as "D. Bland", though only one of them has the correct "W" initial for a second Christian name that matches the inscription found on the memorial. Closer examination of the personal details held for each "D. Bland" also indicates that this same man, Dennis Walter Bland, was linked to the local area by stating that he was the 18 year old *"Son of Bernard Eric and Alice Mary Bland, of Chesterfield, Derbyshire."* Whilst this is not a direct link to the parish, similar research undertaken concerning each of the other five possibilities failed to establish that any of them had any connection with Derbyshire.

A search of the registration data reveals that Dennis had his birth recorded in the Chesterfield district during the March ¼ of 1924, and this same source also confirms that the maiden name of his mother had been Parkes. This added detail therefore allows us to find the record of her marriage to Bernard, and discover that this event had also been recorded in the Chesterfield district during the March ¼ of the previous year. The 1939 Register confirms that his parents were then living at an address in Sutton Springs Wood.

Returning to the records held by the Commonwealth War Grave Commission for details of his service and loss provides us with the information that, numbered as P/JX 163330, he had held the rating of Ordinary Signalman in the Royal Navy. In addition to this we also find that he had been serving aboard H.M.S. Hermes when his life had been lost on 9th April 1942. The fact that he is remembered on the naval memorial at Portsmouth indicates that he has no known grave but the sea, and the reason that he is commemorated there in preference to elsewhere confirms (along with the "P" prefix to his service number) that this had been his home port.

Unfortunately, we do not know when Dennis joined H.M.S. Hermes, though given his young age, it was probably not too long prior to her loss. This ship was actually the first purpose-built vessel to be designed and commissioned as an aircraft carrier, and had first come into service in the same year that he had been born. Despite having undergone several refits over the course of her life that had been intended to keep her in operational service, in 1938, she had officially become a training ship. The outbreak of war, however, saw her once more pressed into active service for which, following another round of refitting in South Africa, she was sent to join the Eastern Fleet.

In April 1942, Hermes was undergoing further work at Trincomalee in Ceylon (now Sri Lanka) that was intended to allow her to play a role in the forthcoming landings at Madagascar. However, Intelligence was received that a Japanese attack on this base was imminent. Despite having none of her aircraft aboard at the time, but in order to avoid being trapped and destroyed in the confines of the port, she put to sea in an attempt to evade the enemy. Unfortunately, she was spotted by a reconnaissance aircraft from the Japanese Battleship Haruna, which forced her to change course and head back under the protection of air cover that could be scrambled from the mainland. She did not, however, manage to make it back under the full umbrella of that air support before she became a target.

On the 9th April, the Japanese launched a major aerial assault from their own aircraft carriers which saw a force of 85 dive bombers head towards the Hermes. Attacked by around 32 of these aircraft, the carrier was actually hit 40 times, and as a result of this furious onslaught both She and her Australian escort Destroyer (H.M.A.S. Vampire) were sunk very quickly. Though many of her complement were actually saved, Dennis was killed in this action along with over 300 others that had been aboard the ill-fated Hermes. Her wreck was discovered in 2006, lying at a depth of around 31 fathoms, about 5 miles off the Eastern shores of Sri Lanka.

WINNARD, H.

HARRY WINNARD

The records of the Commonwealth War Graves Commission return only one result for a casualty of the Second World War when a search is conducted for "H. Winnard". Further information that they hold for him, however, initially fails to make this identification absolutely certain by informing us that he had been the *"Son of Charles and Mary Winnard; husband of Joan Winnard, of Dunnington, Yorkshire."*

Fortunately, subsequent searches of the Derbyshire Times provided the required evidence of his connection to the parish via an obituary that they printed for him on 12th March 1943. Not only does this source connect him to a *"Mrs Winnard of Dunnington"*, but additionally informs us that his parents were at that time residing at 20, Markham Road, Duckmanton. The obituary also adds other details to his story, by telling us that he had been working at *"Markham Deep Hard Colliery"* before he had enlisted in April 1938, well before war had been declared.

A search of the registration data for the entire nation reveals that, by a strange coincidence, two men of this name had their births recorded in the March ¼ of 1920. One of them was registered in the Worksop district and the other in Middlesbro'. Fortunately, this can quickly be resolved by consulting the registration data for the marriages of their parents. One of these shows that a Charles Winnard had married a Mary Rhodes in the September ¼ of 1910, and that the event had been recorded in the Chesterfield district. Conclusively, Mary's maiden name matches that shown for the mother on the birth record of the Harry Winnard that had been registered in Worksop.

We are also fortunate concerning the details of Harry's own wedding, as only one groom of this name had married a bride named Joan within the right time frame. Her maiden name had been Smith, and the event was registered in the Howden district during the December ¼ of 1940. Further circumstantial support for this being the correct marriage record also comes from the fact that Dunnington lay within the Howden registration district at that date.

By the time of his death on 10th February 1943, we know the then 23 year old Harry, numbered as 320389, was serving as a corporal with the 1st King's Dragoon Guards. An old cavalry regiment of the British Army that could trace its origins back to 1685, they had only exchanged their horses for armour as recently as 1937, and two years later, had become a part of the Royal Armoured Corps.

Beginning their wartime service equipped with Vickers-Armstrongs Mk VI B Light Tanks, the regiment did not go overseas until they embarked at Liverpool on 16th November 1940. The long voyage that then lay ahead of them was broken by a short stay in the South African port of Durban, after which they continued on to Egypt where their main body disembarked at Port Said on 30th December. Though we cannot be certain that Harry was with them on that date, he was destined to lose his life in this same theatre of war with them just over 2 years later. By that time, his regiment had seen a great deal of action, having been involved in both the siege and relief of Tobruk, Gazala, Bir Hacheim, the defence of the Alamein Line, Alam Halfa and the advance on Tripoli.

It was only very shortly after their arrival in North Africa, however, that the role of the 1st King's Dragoon Guards underwent a major change. In the first month of 1941, their old Vickers-Armstrongs light tanks were replaced by new vehicles that heralded their conversion into an armoured car regiment. Effectively exchanging tracks for tyres, they were re-equipped with the South African made Marmon Harringtons whose design had been based on a Ford truck chassis. It is most likely that Harry was killed in one of these vehicles, though his unit also had a few Daimler and A.E.C. armoured cars by the time of his death.

Thanks to the excellent records of the 1st Queens Dragoon Guards (the new unit formed by the amalgamation of the King's Dragoon Guards with the Queen's Bays in 1959), we have some further details about Harry's death. Having been withdrawn for rest and maintenance after Tripoli had fallen to the British, from 3rd February the regiment became involved in a further advance on the Southern flank. Seeing action against the Germans from the 5th February, but continuing to push forwards, the regiment crossed into Tunisia on the following day. From the 7th onwards, however, their patrols brought them into almost constant contact with both enemy ground forces and the dive-bombers of the Luftwaffe. On the 10th February, Harry's armoured car was hit by enemy fire, killing him and wounding both Trooper McAleavey and the vehicle's commander Lieutenant Phillips.

Regrettably, Harry has no known grave, and is therefore commemorated at the Alamein Memorial in Egypt, which is many miles distant from the place where he actually fell.

CURRY, T.

THOMAS EDMUND CURRY

The records of the Commonwealth War Graves Commission return a list of seven casualties of the Second World War when a search is conducted for casualties that might match the name of the "T. Curry" that is inscribed on the memorial. We are, however, fortunate that the personal information given for one of these makes a direct link to the parish and therefore establishes his identity beyond doubt. This record describes Thomas, perhaps a little confusingly, as being the *"Son of Clement Watkinson, and of Rebecca Watkinson, of Arkwright Town, Derbyshire."* In addition, it goes on to inform us that he had been 25 years of age when he lost his life in 1943, and therefore also provided enough detail for us to begin to investigate his origins.

The registration records add to our knowledge by showing that his birth had been recorded in the Chesterfield district during the December ¼ of 1917. It is interesting to note, however, that the surname of his mother is also declared to have been Curry on this document. This confusion takes on new levels of complexity when the marriage record for his parents is discovered. It was registered in the same district during the December ¼ of 1918 but, whilst it clearly names the groom as Clement Watkinson, it refers to his bride as having been Rebecca Kerry. There is, however, little doubt that this is the correct record, because no other registration document exists that was made between the years of 1875 and 1945 for a Clement Watkinson that had a wife with maiden name of Curry.

The 1939 Register shows the family living at 72, Arkwright Town, and describes Thomas as having then been a *"Surface Worker"*, thereby indicating that he was involved in the local mining industry. A marriage record has also been discovered in the Chesterfield district, which was registered in the March ¼ of 1942, where the groom was a Thomas Curry and his bride is identified as having been a Joan Needham. Additionally, a birth record registered in the same district during the March ¼ of 1943 has also been found, which informs us of the arrival of a daughter into this family named Judith. Although these are highly likely to relate to this same Thomas, no firm evidence has been found which allows us to establish that connection with 100% certainty. This is, however, the only birth record that exists for a child with the surname Curry who had a mother with the maiden name of Needham.

What we know with certainty, from the records of the Commonwealth War Graves Commission, is that Thomas (serving with the number 4979067), was a Private in the 6th Battalion of the Lincolnshire Regiment at the time of his death. This was another unit of the Territorial Army that had its origins in the decision that was taken to double the strength of that entire organisation as a pre-war precaution. As a formation of the 138th Infantry Brigade within the 46th Infantry Division, they were sent to join the British Expeditionary Force in France towards the end of April 1940. Despite being designated as a labour and training unit, they suffered badly at the hands of the advancing Germans until they were eventually evacuated from Dunkirk. Once back in Britain, the entire Division was forced to undergo an extensive period of rebuilding, training and re-equipping, and they were subsequently assigned home defence duties until the threat of a German invasion had receded sufficiently for them to be deployed on any further service overseas. It is likely that Thomas first joined them as a conscript during this period.

It was not until January of 1943 that the 46th Division left Britain for a second time, when they were deployed to play an active role in the final part of the North African Campaign. They were actually a formation of the 1st Army in North Africa and not the perhaps more famous 8th, though both of these forces were involved in the action in which it is believed that Thomas was killed.

With all their other key objectives secured, the Allies at last turned their attention towards launching a major offensive designed to capture the city of Tunis, the last stronghold of the Axis forces in North Africa. By this time all of the enemy's forces had already been hemmed into a small corner of land with the sea at their backs, and with the Allies also having previously established air superiority to prevent their being either reinforced or re-supplied, the process of tightening the noose around that city had already begun. It was on the morning of the 22nd April, the first day of that offensive, that Thomas's 46th Division began its part in the attack by creating a gap in the enemy defences through which the 6th Armoured Corps could pass. Sadly, as the Axis powers met this attack with dogged resistance, this was also destined to be the day on which Thomas would lose his life. After a long and bitter struggle their enemies were, however, eventually forced to yield, and British tanks entered Tunis on the 7th May. Within a few days of that the Axis forces finally surrendered, and around 230,000 of them became prisoners of war.

Thomas is buried at the Medjez-el-Bab War Cemetery, which lies about 37 miles to the West of Tunis.

BRYON, R. W.

ROBERT WILLIAM BRYON

The records of the Commonwealth War Graves Commission contain only one record for a casualty of the Second World War that was named "R. Bryon." This identification is, however, further endorsed because their records confirm that the initial of his second Christian name stood for William, and thereby provide us with an exact match for the inscription of "R. W. Bryon" that appears on the memorial. Additional personal information is also available from this source, which in describing him as the *"Son of Albert Bryon, and of Edith Mary Bryon, of Duckmanton, Derbyshire."*, also neatly establishes his connection with the parish.

Other data gathered from the records of the Commonwealth War Graves Commission soon led us to an obituary that was printed for him in the Derbyshire Times on the 21st May 1943. This adds yet more detail to the information that we already have for Robert by indicating that he had worked at Markham Colliery before joining the army, and also dates his enlistment to having occurred in either October or November 1940. Perhaps a little confusingly, however, it also describes his mother as having been *"Mrs E. M. Spacie of 16, North Grove, Duckmanton,"*, and is therefore slightly at odds with the information contained in the War Graves records.

Fortunately, the registration data comes to our aid in addressing this issue, not only by showing that Robert's birth had been recorded in the Chesterfield district during the March ¼ of 1921, but by also revealing that the maiden name of his mother had been Boulton. This new piece of information enabled us to identify the record for the marriage of his parents, which had been made in the same district during the previous year, and the discovery of which simultaneously confirmed another statement made in his obituary telling us that Robert had been her eldest son. Confirmation of the untimely death of his father, Albert Bryon, at the age of just 43, was found in a third record that was made during the September ¼ of 1936, whilst a fourth document from the same source then showed that Edith had found happiness again when, just over 4 years later, she had married Joseph Spacie during the December ¼ of 1940.

Returning to the Commonwealth War Graves Commission for information on his military service, we were informed that Robert had died at the age of 22 whilst numbered as 2621724 and serving as a Guardsman with the 5th Battalion of the Grenadier Guards. This was a wartime raised unit of the regiment which, though originally only having three battalions, went on to double its strength to six during the course of the conflict. The 3rd, 5th and 6th Battalions all served in the North Africa Campaign as part of the First Army, where Robert's 5th Battalion served as a unit of 24th Guards Brigade in the 1st Infantry Division.

Departing in late February of 1943, the 5th Battalion arrived in Algiers on 9th March, but were soon on the move again both by boat and overland to Tunisia. By 19th March they were in the front line in the hills overlooking Oued Zagga, and it was here that they sustained their first casualties before moving on to Medjez el Bab ten days later. They were destined to spend longer here, and soon began the business of strengthening their defensive positions in a place that was actually known as Grenadiers Hill. This was a relatively quiet period for Robert's battalion, though they did sustain more casualties when conducting night time patrols in no man's land. This activity was, however, considered important, because they knew it was likely that they would be required to push forward over this ground when an impending Allied offensive in that area got underway.

Unfortunately, the Germans were not ignorant of these Allied plans, and launched an attack of their own in this area on 20th April that they hoped would disrupt their enemies' forthcoming offensive. The Grenadiers were, however, supported by Churchill tanks, which on this occasion proved to be more than a match for the German armour that advanced towards them. By dawn of the following day, the situation was under control, and the enemy attack had been repulsed. Fortunately, the Grenadiers were only on the fringes of this action and therefore suffered relatively light casualties that amounted to 5 killed and 12 wounded. Falling far short of achieving its desired objective, this failed German initiative did not even delay the start of the British attack.

When the British offensive was launched on 23rd April, the objectives of Robert's battalion centred around the capture of a piece of high ground that was known as "Point 134." Together with another feature known as "Hill Ridiculous" (which was to be attacked by other battalions from within their brigade), these would become the key points in what later became known in the Guards history of the conflict as the Battle of The Bou. Advancing under cover of darkness in the early hours, the Grenadiers faced little opposition until, close to their goal, the full fury of their covering creeping artillery barrage began to land on the objective that lay just ahead of them. Even then, the resistance they encountered was patchy. In some areas their enemies surrendered almost immediately, whilst other positions were only carried by using grenades and the points of their bayonets. Most of the defenders here were actually Tunisian Frenchmen who had been recruited to serve under German command. Once all resistance had been overcome and Point 134 had been secured, some of the Grenadiers were detailed to continue their advance. Though this was largely a mopping up operation aimed at clearing the enemy from ground adjacent to the nearby village of Grich el Oued, it once again, however, saw them become involved in another sharp though fortunately brief and one-sided fire fight.

Whilst his obituary states that Robert was killed in action on 23rd April, it remains possible that he could actually have died of wounds received before the battalion's involvement in the action around Point 134. His final resting place is at the Massicault War Cemetery, which lies approximately 19 miles to the South West of Tunis, though the records of the Commonwealth War Graves Commission show that he was originally buried elsewhere and that his remains were re-interred there on 1st August 1943.

MADIN, R.

ROY WRIGHT MADIN

We were fortunate that the records of the Commonwealth War Graves Commission returned only one result for a casualty of WW2 when a search was conducted for "R. Madin." However, the personal information that they hold for him merely states that he was the *"Husband of Dorothy May Madin, of Chesterfield, Derbyshire"*, and whilst this did at least link this casualty to the local area, it disappointingly failed to provide the required evidence of any direct connection with the parish of Sutton-cum-Duckmanton. These same records did, however, contain the extra details that this man, numbered as 5887838, had been serving as a Corporal with the 2nd Battalion of the Northamptonshire Regiment when his life was lost on 11th July 1943 at the age of 26. In addition, this was also the first source to intimate that his full name had been Roy Wright Madin.

The Derbyshire Times published an obituary for Roy on 13th August 1943, which added a little more to our knowledge by linking him to an address of 130, Derby Road, Chesterfield. Further information disclosed in this source also began to bring his story a little closer to the parish by stating that, before his marriage in February of 1942, he had lived with his parents at an address given as Belvoir, Temple Normanton. An inspection of the memorials in that parish, however, revealed that his name had not been remembered there, and it therefore seems possible that his parents may either have moved into Sutton-cum Duckmanton before the WW2 inscriptions were added to those memorials, or that their property had actually lain on the Sutton-cum-Duckmanton side of the parish boundary.

An interrogation of the registration data confirmed the existence of a marriage record for Roy that was made in the Chesterfield district during the March ¼ of 1942, which showed that his wife's maiden name had been Spencer. Furthermore, a unique birth record also exists for a Roy W. Madin that was made in the March ¼ of 1917, showing that his mother's maiden name had been Barber. Interestingly, this record was actually made in the Bakewell district rather than in Chesterfield. Continuing to search these data subsequently revealed that his parents were named Roger and Ellen, and that they had been married in the Chesterfield district during the June ¼ of 1915. Little is known of Roy's early life, but his obituary states that he had been employed at the Goods Yard of the London Midland and Scottish Railway in Chesterfield before he joined the army in February of 1940.

We have no clear understanding of his army life before the date of his death, but for the entire war, the 2nd Battalion served as part of the 17th Infantry Brigade in the 5th Infantry Division. They were first sent to France with the original British Expeditionary Force, but after their subsequent evacuation from Dunkirk, they spent a long period in England. On 5th May of 1942 (by which time Roy is likely to have been with them), they landed to take part in the successful Battle of Madagascar, which liberated that island from the rule of Vichy France. Becoming widely travelled after that, they went on to serve in India, Persia (modern Iran), Iraq and Egypt.

It was during the early stages of the Allied landing on Sicily (codenamed Operation Husky) that Roy would lose his life. The port of Syracuse was captured on the 10th July, the day before his death, and it is in Syracuse War Cemetery, about 2 miles to the West of the port, that his remains were interred and he receives his official commemoration.

MOORE, W.

CHARLES WILLIAM MOORE

The records of the Commonwealth War Graves Commission hold many entries for casualties of the Second World War that fit the inscription we have on the memorial for "W. Moore." Indeed, if we include those with extra initials for second or third Christian names, there are actually 129 of them. Interestingly, however, it is the record of a man who would more accurately have been described as "C. Moore" that immediately attracted our attention. We have no matching inscription for this man on the memorial, and yet their records clearly describe him as being the *"Son of Fred and Elizabeth Moore of Duckmanton, Derbyshire."* There are several explanations for this apparent discrepancy, the first and most obvious of which being that the memorial inscription may simply be incorrect. The casualty with this documented Duckmanton connection was actually Charles William Moore, making it possible that the engravers had inadvertently omitted his first initial. Another possibility is that, despite being named as Charles William, this man was more familiarly known to his friends and family by his second Christian name. This is, after all, quite a commonly encountered scenario. A third possibility, of course, is that there was no attempt to commemorate Charles William on the memorial, and that the inscription relates to a completely different individual. This, however, would seem to be the most unlikely explanation of them all.

Whilst the discrepancy concerning this man's initials may seem a minor concern, it does, however, introduce sufficient element of doubt to this identification that it should only stand as "probable" rather than be considered "certain". As no local obituary has been traced for any man of either name, and no entry located in the 1939 Register, the absolute confirmation of this attribution is not likely to come from any of the written records that are currently available in the public domain.

Continuing with the likelihood that the inscription on the memorial was intended to commemorate Charles William Moore, we can establish from the records of the Commonwealth War Graves Commission that he was 23 years old when his life was lost on 24th August 1943. However, owing to there being multiple matching entries for the registration of births of men named Charles Moore, it has unfortunately been impossible to be certain which of these records relate to this specific individual. From the inscription that appears on his headstone, however, we do know that he had a brother and at least two sisters.

Turning to his military service, we know that Charles, numbered as 937174, was a Sergeant (Flight Engineer) with 78 Squadron. This was a unit that had its origins in the Great War with the Royal Flying Corps, though during that era it had been equipped with fighter aircraft and employed defending the South Coast of Britain. This original incarnation of 78 Squadron was, however, disbanded on the last day of 1919, a few months after the signing of the peace treaty at Versailles had brought that conflict to an end.

A gap of almost seventeen years then ensued until the RAF, beginning to build up its strength as another European crisis loomed, reformed the Squadron at the end of 1936. The original nucleus for its new incarnation came from 10 Squadron, who were equipped with Handley Page biplanes that would doubtless have looked familiar to those who had flown with the squadron in the Great War. There was, however, one key difference, these Heyford aircraft were actually twin engined bombers.

The remaining pre-war years brought several more changes for the recently revived 78 squadron, which saw them both move their base and take delivery of new Armstrong Whitworth Whitley bombers. Indeed, they moved several more times after 3rd September 1939, going first to Linton-on-Ouse in a training role, and then moving to Dishforth as a front-line unit engaged in night bombing. They then went on to see overseas in Malta before returning to Britain to take part in their first bombing raid on

Berlin.

In October 1941, the squadron moved once again, this time to Croft in County Durham, and it was here that they began to receive the new four engined Halifax bombers of the type in which Charles would be killed. Their first operation with these new aircraft was a raid on Ostend on 29th April 1942, and a month after that their aircraft took part in the first "1,000 bomber raid" that devastated Cologne.

After several more moves, 78 Squadron eventually found a home at Breighton in the East Riding of Yorkshire, and it was from here that Charles would set off on his final flight. Taking off at 20:24 hrs on 23rd August 1943 in a Halifax Mk II with the serial number JD248 and EY-J fuselage markings, they were part of an operation that involved a total of 727 aircraft in a raid on Berlin. Despite not going entirely as planned, this would prove to be the most devastating blow dealt to the German capital to date. Not only were many Nazi government buildings badly damaged in this raid, but 20 ships were sunk and 854 people killed.

It was in the small hours of the following day that Charles' Halifax came into the sights of a Messerschmitt Bf 110 G-4 night fighter flown by Unteroffizier Josef Brunner. No account of the aerial combat which ensued has been found, but the Halifax was shot down close to Netzow, around 60 miles to the North West of Berlin. One of her seven man crew, Sergeant D. Lamb, miraculously survived and became a prisoner of war. The other six, including Charles, sadly perished. The British casualties on this particular raid were very heavy indeed, and another four Halifax bombers from 78 Squadron were also lost that night.

On 25th March 1945, during another nighttime mission, Joseph Brunner and the other two members of his aircrew were shot down and killed near Oppenheim.

Charles' final resting place is at the Berlin War Cemetery, where around 80% of the graves are those of fellow airmen who lost their lives in the skies over Germany. It is presumed that he was originally buried elsewhere and that his remains were brought here after the war.

WHARTON, C.

CHARLES WHARTON

Unfortunately, no obituary has been traced for Charles, but the evidence found for him amongst the records of the Commonwealth War Graves Commission is sufficient to establish his identity beyond doubt. Their archives contain details for only 3 men that match the name of "C. Wharton" who were casualties of the Second World War. Of these, only Charles has personal details which establish a connection to the parish. Their records clearly show him to have been the *"Son of Charles and Rhoda Wharton, of Duckmanton, Derbyshire."*, and provide us with the additional information that he had been just 20 years old when his life was lost in 1943.

Once again, these details provide a route into the registration data which both confirm that his birth was recorded in the Chesterfield district during the December ¼ of 1922, and that the maiden name of his mother had been Bower. This additional detail is also sufficient for us to determine that his parents had married in the same district during the December ¼ of 1919. Charles was their only son, but was preceded by his sister Betty who had been born in 1921.

Several other sources have fortunately been located that provide some details concerning his fate. The records of the Commonwealth War Graves Commission show us that he was serving under the number 1031763 as a Sergeant (Air Gunner) with the Royal Air Force Volunteer Reserve at the time of his death, and they also provide us with his unit details, which show that he was flying with 57 Squadron. This was another old formation that had originally been created in 1916 as a training unit of the Royal

Flying Corps, though later they had also gone on to see active service in the skies over France during the Great War.

After war was declared in 1939, the squadron returned to France in a strategic reconnaissance role, though it also gained some bombing experience there before finding itself back in England during May of the following year. Many more changes lay ahead over the following months, with the squadron initially being deployed to Scotland for operations against the Norwegian coast. It was, however, brought back down the country to Feltwell in Norfolk before the end of 1940. Here it was re-equipped with Wellington bombers before, almost 2 years later, it was sent to Scampton and given Lancasters. One final move, in August of 1943, brought the squadron to East Kirkby in Lincolnshire where it would be based for the remaining duration of the war.

Whilst we do not know when Charles joined them, it was from this airfield that he set off on what would be his final flight. Along with the other 6 members of his crew, Charles took off at 17:31 hrs on 20th October 1943 in a Lancaster III with the serial number JB234 and the markings DX-E on its fuselage. For their forthcoming raid on the distant German city of Leipzig, the aircraft of 57 Squadron would actually only form a small contingent of an aerial armada consisting of 358 Lancasters. It is believed that Charles' aircraft was intercepted and shot down by a German night fighter between midnight on 20th October and 01:00 hrs on the 21st, though no corresponding claims have been found to confirm this amongst the files of the Luftwaffe. A total of 16 Lancasters were lost during this raid, and several others that did manage to return are reported to have been damaged when landing.

The wreckage of Charles' aircraft came down in the vicinity of the river Elbe near Arneburg, and sadly, all of its crew are known to have perished. Initially buried in a local cemetery, their bodies were moved after the war and brought to their final resting place at the Berlin 1939-45 War Cemetery. It is interesting to note that another member of the crew of that same Lancaster, Sergeant Cyril Thomas Harston (Air Bomber), was the son of William and Kate Harston of Bolsover, and that he is commemorated on their memorial. He lies just a few short yards away from Charles in that same cemetery.

PECK, G.

GORDON JOSEPH WILLIAM PECK

 Gordon is yet another casualty for which no obituary has been traced, though his identity can be established with certainty via information found in the records of the Commonwealth War Graves Commission. Details that they hold declare him to have been the *"Son of George Walter and Doris Peck, of Duckmanton, Derbyshire; husband of Marjorie Peck."*

Given that these records also show that he was just 19 years of age when he lost his life in 1944, his unique name and initials readily enable us to identify that the registration of his birth took place in the Chesterfield district during the December ¼ of 1924. The information that the maiden name of his mother had been Shelton is also shown on this record, allowing for an additional search to be made that enables us to find the details of his parent's marriage. This was also recorded in the Chesterfield district during the December ¼ of 1921.

Having such a unique combination of names also allows us to find the details of Gordon's own marriage with ease. This event, again recorded in the Chesterfield district during the December ¼ of 1942, shows the maiden name of his bride to have been Wall. Subsequent searches of birth records also reveal evidence to indicate that the couple went on to have to have children before Gordon was killed.

The records of the Commonwealth War Graves Commission also provide us with some basic information concerning Gordon's time in the military by showing that, numbered as 1812386, he had been serving as a Sergeant (Flight Engineer) with the Royal Air Force Volunteer Reserve when his life was lost. The same source also provides us with his unit details, which show that he had been serving with 51 Squadron.

This squadron began its life as a home defence unit in May of 1916, and was therefore initially equipped with fighter aircraft and deployed in an air-to-air combat role. Later, towards the end of the Great War, it was converted into a training unit before the cessation of those hostilities ultimately led to it being disbanded in June 1919. They were, however, reformed as a bomber unit in 1937 from a nucleus that had been transferred from 58 Squadron. The squadron witnessed quite a few changes after war had been declared which, during 1942, even included a spell with Coastal Command engaged against German U-Boats. All of this, however, would doubtless have taken place before Gordon had joined them.

The squadron moved to a new home at Snaith in the East Riding of Yorkshire when it was transferred back to Bomber Command in October 1942. It was shortly after its arrival here that it was re-equipped with Halifax bombers, and it was whilst taking part in an operation aboard one of these aircraft in April 1944 that Gordon would be killed.

With the serial number LV880 and fuselage marking of MH-C, the Halifax Mk III on which Gordon would make his final flight took off from Snaith at 21:20 hrs on 10th April 1944. Carrying 7 x 1000 and 6 x 500 pound bombs, her seven man crew set out on an operation that would target the important railway yards at Tergnier in Northern France. This was quite a large raid involving 157 Halifax's and 10 Mosquito Pathfinders in the main attack, whilst a further 36 Mosquitoes conducted a diversionary raid on Hannover. Despite the fact that this diversion seems to have drawn some of the German night-fighters away from the vicinity of the main target, 10 of the Halifax's that took part in the larger raid were destined not to return.

Amongst the German night-fighters that were sent up to intercept them that night was a twin engined Messerschmitt Bf 110 piloted by Hauptmann Gerhard Freidrich. Already an ace with eleven "victories" to his credit, he singled out Gordon's aircraft and attacked at just after midnight. The combat took place at an altitude of 10,500 feet in the skies above Montdidier, and resulted in the port wing of the Halifax being set alight. In an attempt to save his aircraft, Pilot Officer Horace Mervyn Hall put the plane into a steep dive in a desperate bid to extinguish the flames. Unfortunately, this did not have the desired result, and realising that it was hopeless, he next issued the order for the crew to bail out. Before any aboard had the opportunity to react to this, however, the Halifax exploded. Miraculously, three members of her crew were blown clear of the wreckage by the force of that explosion, and somehow managed to survive, but Gordon was not amongst their number and sadly perished along with Hall and the two other men who had been onboard. The remains of all 4 of the fatalities from Gordon's Halifax are interred at Davenescourt Communal Cemetery in the Somme region of France.

We are also able to provide a brief but perhaps interesting post-script to Gordon's story. On the night of 16th March 1945, Gerhard Freidrich, by then with 32 victories to his credit, also became one of the vanquished when his Junkers 88 collided with a Lancaster near Stuttgart. There were no survivors from either of the two aircraft that were involved.

PENNEY, J.

JOHN W. PENNEY

The identification of this casualty has only been confirmed by a process that has involved connecting several strands of evidence. These investigations have, however, revealed that this man is also remembered on the memorial in neighbouring Calow, though his name appears there in a slightly different format.

Starting with the records of the Commonwealth War Graves Commission, we discovered that there are just four possibilities for casualties of the Second World War who could be a match for the inscription of "J. Penney." Our interest, however, is soon drawn to just one of these men who they name as John. He is shown to have been numbered as 4864487, and to have held the rank of Lance Sergeant with the 7th Battalion of the Leicestershire Regiment. The additional information that they hold for him also states that he had been the *"son of Charles and Lucy Penney; husband of Jane Penney, of Calow, Derbyshire."*, supplying us with an immediate local connection. Frustratingly, this evidence falls short of providing any details that establish any direct link with Sutton-cum-Duckmanton, and as no obituary could be located for John in the local press, the initial prospects of making such a connection looked bleak. This was, however, resolved by the discovery of a small personal advertisement that was placed in the Derbyshire Times on 16th June 1944. Containing very few words it simply stated that:

"Mrs Penney, Meadow Cottage, Duckmanton, would like to thank

relatives and friends for the kind expressions of sympathy in the loss of her dear son, L./Sgt John W. Penney."

It was only after this vital fragment of evidence had made that connection to the parish that it became possible to conduct meaningful searches of the registration data, and it was amongst these records where it was discovered that John had married Lucy Willis in the Chesterfield district during the September ¼ of 1935. Other evidence was also found here showing that the couple had gone on to have two sons named Jack and David who had been born in 1936 and 1939 respectively but that, sadly, David had died during the third ¼ of 1942. More records also emerged from this same source, including a birth record for John that was made in the Chesterfield district during the September ¼ of 1910, and a marriage record for his parents that was also made in the same district during 1909. This informed us that his father was Charles Horace Penney, and that the full maiden name of his mother had been Lucy Ann Rowlett.

Having established all of these details about his family, it is of interest to note that the memorial at Calow carries an inscription for *"Jack Penny, 7ᵗʰ Leics."*. There are, however, several reasons why this must have been intended to be a commemoration of the same man. Not least of these is the more than coincidental reference to the 7ᵗʰ Battalion of the Leicestershire Regiment, though there are others. Importantly, there is simply no record of any man named Jack Penny having lost his life in the Second World War. "Jack" is therefore almost certainly a familiar or pet name by which he was known to his wife in their family home at Calow. In addition to this, there is actually not one single casualty of the conflict who is recorded as having been a "J. Penny." The engraving of the surname with that spelling at Calow would therefore seem to be a simple error.

The 7ᵗʰ Battalion of the Leicestershire Regiment was not part of the pre-war establishment of the Regular British Army, but was raised in Nottingham in July 1940 for wartime service. By that date, the evacuation of the British Expeditionary Force from Dunkirk and the Fall of France had increased the likelihood of a German invasion of Britain, and this new battalion was therefore originally embodied for the purpose of home defence. From the records of the Leicestershire Regiment, we know that John enlisted on 17ᵗʰ July

1940, and that he is therefore likely to have been a founder member of this unit.

His battalion remained in Britain until September 1942 when, with the threat of invasion having subsided, they were sent to India. The following year, however, they saw another change in their deployment when they were assigned to join the Chindits. A remarkable and unique formation with a highly specialist function, they were a long-range penetration force that was specifically developed to be deployed behind enemy lines. Once established in strongpoints that were located deep within the Japanese held jungles of Burma, their role became one of disrupting and weakening their enemy from within.

John's battalion, as a formation of the 14th Infantry Brigade, took part in the infamous 2nd Chindit which was codenamed Operation Thursday. Initially under the leadership of the charismatic but highly eccentric Orde Wingate, this particular sortie coincided with a major Japanese invasion of North East India. The specialist and somewhat irregular Allied Chindit force successfully disrupted the supply lines that were supporting this enemy advance and also tied up troops that the Japanese could otherwise have sent to bolster their invasion attempt. Though still the subject of debate, the role of the Chindits in diverting the attention of the enemy away from their front was probably a key factor behind the ultimate failure of this Japanese incursion into India. The costs, however, in terms of the casualties sustained by the Chindits, were horrendous. In addition to the losses that they incurred through enemy action, an extremely high proportion of their men suffered terribly from the effects of both tropical diseases and malnutrition. Indeed, the casualty rate amongst the 7th Battalion of the Leicestershire Regiment proved to be so great that they were disbanded after the conclusion of Operation Thursday. The few men of John's old unit who were still considered fit for active duty were at that point transferred to the 2nd Battalion of the regiment.

We know, again from the records of the Leicestershire Regiment, that John was killed in action on 13th May 1944 at the age of 33. Interred now at the Taukkyan War Cemetery at Yangon (formerly Rangoon) in Myanmar (formerly Burma), his remains were exhumed from their original resting place and taken there for reburial after the war had ended.

GLENN, E.

EDWARD GLENN

Sadly, the identity of the man commemorated on the memorial by the inscription "E. GLENN" cannot be fully confirmed, because no firm evidence has been found that makes a definite connection between any specific individual serviceman and the parish. However, the circumstantial evidence discovered that justifies this therefore tentative attribution remains compelling. Starting with the records of the Commonwealth War Graves Commission, we found that only 4 people with this combination of initial and surname are listed as having been casualties of the Second World War. Initially, therefore, we were faced with a process of elimination in order to try and establish which of these alternatives would be the most likely to have been commemorated at Sutton-cum-Duckmanton.

Edward was the man at the head of this list of search results, though the additional family details that were shown for him offered little immediate encouragement by declaring him to have been the *"Son of Frank and Jessie Glenn; husband of Mary Ellen Glenn, of Clerkenwell, London."* Additional information provided by this source, which informs us that he had been just 24 years old at the time of his death, would, however, prove to be significant as our investigation progressed.

Consulting the country-wide registration data for the years 1880 – 1922 in search of marriages between a Frank Glenn and a bride that had the Christian name of Jessie returns only one matching record. This not only reveals that her maiden surname had been Colls, but perhaps more significantly, shows that this unique event had been registered in the Chesterfield district during the December ¼ of 1917. We have therefore at least established a link for this man to the local area if not directly to the parish.

Returning to the Commonwealth War Graves information, the detail that Edward was declared to have been 24 years old when he died on 7th June 1944, provides us with sufficient reason for an additional meaningful search of the registration data to be conducted. For this to have been the case he must have been born somewhere between 8th June 1919 and 6th June 1921. Returning to the countrywide data, a wider ranging search for a matching birth record between December 1918 and March 1922 finds just two results. Only one of these relates to a mother who had the maiden name Colls, and this was again recorded in the Chesterfield district during the September ¼ of 1919. This search result is also a perfect match for the age at death given for Edward in the war graves records. A further wide-ranging search, aimed at finding a record for Edward's own marriage, again reveals only one positive result in the entire country for the period March 1935 to December 1947. With his bride identified as Mary E. Cleary, this event was also recorded in the Chesterfield district, during the December ¼ of 1943.

Given that the dates of all of the events that have already been discovered fall well after the 1911 Census, the data that this source contains is only of limited value. It does, however, show that both a Frank Glenn and a Jessie Colls were living in the Chesterfield area at that time, though neither of them had any obvious connection to Sutton-cum-Duckmanton at this earlier date.

The records of the Commonwealth War Graves Commission that give us details of his service show that Edward was a member of a highly specialised force, the 22nd Independent Company of the Parachute Regiment. This was a small "pathfinder" unit whose role called for them to be dropped behind enemy lines in order to prepare a scheduled landing site ahead of the arrival of a full-scale airborne assault. As can be expected of a group with such a niche purpose, its structure was very different to that found in the rest of the army. It consisted of only around 132 men of all ranks, and was subdivided into 4 platoons. One of these acted as a Headquarters unit, whilst the remaining 3 were each further subdivided into 3 "sticks", each of which came under the leadership of a Corporal or

Sergeant. As a Lance Corporal, Edward therefore held an important role in the command structure of his stick.

The 22nd Independent Company was formed between May and September of 1943 for service with the deceptively named 6th Airborne Division. Though there was a 1st Airborne Division, the 6th was actually only the second such unit, and had been allotted that higher number purely to encourage the Germans into believing that there were actually another 5 similar formations in existence.

Taking off from RAF Harwell at around midnight on 5th June 1944, Edward's stick was flown in a twin engined Armstrong Whitworth Albemarle aircraft from 295 Squadron. In the early hours of the following morning, they were dropped from 500 feet onto their landing area to the East of Caen, putting them amongst the very first Allied troops that set foot on French soil during the Normandy landings of 1944. Once arrived they would have secured their landing area, and should then have begun to set up ground-to-air radio beacons that were to be used to guide elements of the 6th Airborne Division onto the drop zone that had been selected for their landing. Unfortunately, they were unable to complete this task, as all of their beacons had either been lost or damaged during their own landing. They were, however, more successful after the main body of the 6th Airborne had arrived, and managed to join up with them prior to their planned assault on the German coastal battery at Merville. Elements from the larger force of 6th Airborne were tasked with destroying these fortified German gun emplacements as part of Operation Tonga, designed to secure strategic objectives and neutralise enemy strong-points that lay ahead of the troops that were to be landed on the invasion beaches. The battery at Merville was considered to be of particular importance because its field of fire actually covered the Sword invasion beach.

Whilst the exact circumstances of Edward's death, less than 2 days after he had parachuted into France, are unknown, some sources have been discovered that describe him as having been killed in action. His final resting place is perhaps fittingly in the Churchyard at Ranville, which holds the distinction of being the first village that was liberated in the whole of France. Its deliverance came in the early hours of 6th June, at the hands of the 6th Airborne division in which Edward had served.

CROOKES, J.

JOHN CROOK

It is likely that the true identity of the man commemorated on memorial by the inscription "Crookes, J" would not have been established had it not been for the discovery of a 5-line notice that appeared in the Derbyshire Times on 28th July 1944. The finding of this evidence would, however, prove crucial in bringing to light another spelling error on the memorial.

The CWGC records contain only one record for a man that matches the memorial inscription, providing us with the details that he had lost his life on 4th June 1944 whilst serving as a Private with the 2nd/4th Battalion of the King's Own Yorkshire Light Infantry. Unfortunately, it contains no additional information regarding either his family or origins, making it all too easy to conclude that he must, therefore, be the man who is commemorated at Sutton-cum-Duckmanton. The notice that was discovered in the Derbyshire Times, however, obviously relates to a completely different individual with a slightly different surname. The CWGC records for a Lance Sergeant named John Crook could easily have been overlooked, but hold information that describes him as being the *"Son of John and Edith Selina Crook; husband of Edith May Crook, of Carr Vale, Derbyshire."* Whilst this obviously shows a local connection for this man it still, however, falls short of establishing a direct link with the parish. Fortunately, the notice printed in the Derbyshire Times fills this void by being worded:

CROOK. – Memories of our dear son-in-law, L./Sgt J. Crook, died of wounds, Italy, June 27th, 1944. "Midst smiles and tears we will always think of you." All at 126, Arkwright Town."

With his date of death, place of burial and rank exactly matching those details given for John Crook by the Commonwealth War Graves Commission, and his connection to the parish also now established, we can be certain that he was actually the man that the memorial inscription had been intended to commemorate.

This discovery allows us to search the registration data, where we find the record of his marriage to Edith May. This was made in the Chesterfield district in the September ¼ of 1933, and reveals that her maiden name had been Alvey. Unfortunately, no direct connection has been found to link her with Joseph Kirby Alvey who features elsewhere in these pages, though it does still remain possible that they were related. With regard to John's birth, we are sadly less fortunate, as a wide-ranging search reveals no results for anyone with this name in the Chesterfield district. We are, therefore, unable to determine which of the many matching countrywide records actually relate to him, and are similarly therefore unable to cast any light upon where his parents had been married.

John, numbered as 4970135, was serving with the 4th Regiment of the Reconnaissance Corps when his life was lost at the age of 34. This is another unusual unit that did not exist in Britain's pre-war Regular Army, and similar to the origins of the Machine Gun Corps in the Great War era, it was created as a direct response to the fighting that had been experienced during the early days of this later conflict. Officially formed in January of 1941, its units were originally styled as "Battalions" in the Infantry tradition and used the numbers of the Divisions in which they served. This was, however, changed in June 1942 when the Corps universally adopted the nomenclature of the Cavalry and saw their "Battalions" become re-styled as "Regiments." In 1944 the Corps was absorbed into the Royal Armoured Corps and, again mirroring the fate of the Machine Gun Corps from that earlier generation, was actually disbanded in 1946 after the hostilities had ceased.

We do not know if John's military service started before the formation of his Reconnaissance unit, though much of the original manpower for his 4th Regiment of the Corps came from the anti-tank companies that already existed in the Brigades of the 4th Division. The first overseas service of this new unit began in North Africa in 1943, where as a unit of IX Corps with the First Army, they helped to gain the final victory over the Axis forces in Tunisia in May of that year.

Their next deployment took them to Italy in February 1944, where they became a unit of the British X Corps. In March, however, they transferred to XIII Corps who were part of the Eighth Army, and it was whilst serving with his unit as part of this larger force that John's life was lost. One of the additional sources that have been identified informs us that he died of wounds received from shell fire, though frustratingly we do not know exactly where or when those fatal injuries were received. It is, however, likely that he was wounded in June during the battle for the German held Trasimene Line, where XIII Corps had faced the might of the German LXXVI Panzer Corps.

John's final resting place is at the Assisi War Cemetery in the Province of Perugia, Italy, which lies approximately 80 miles to the North of Rome.

CLARKE, B.

BADEN CLARKE

Unsurprisingly, there are several men listed in the records of the Commonwealth War Graves Commission who would match the inscription on the memorial for "B. Clarke." Baden's record, however, is the only one which contains personal details that provide evidence of a direct link to the parish. This additional information describes him as having been the *"Son of Thomas and Alice Clarke, of Duckmanton, Derbyshire"*, and from another source, we have been able to discover that their address was 7, North Road, Duckmanton.

Shown to have been 26 years old at the time of his death on 7th February 1945, his unusual Christian name allows us to both trace the registration of his birth to the Chesterfield district during the September ¼ of 1918 and to establish that his mother's maiden name had been Neale. Having that extra piece of information allowed us to find the register entry for the marriage of his parents, which shows that this event had been recorded in the same district during the June ¼ of 1905. As their marriage pre-dates the 1911 census we are also able to add from that source that Baden's parents were at that time living on Station Road in Brimington, and to discover that his mother had actually been born in that parish whilst his father had originated from Staveley.

Fortunately, though we have no obituary, we do have a brief article about Baden that was published in the Derbyshire Times on 3rd April 1942. This tells us that he had worked at *"Markham Deep Hard Pit"* before being conscripted, and that he had already seen a lot of active service before the date of its publication. We are also told that he had been in France with the British Expeditionary

Force, and that he was fortunate to have been evacuated from Dunkirk before the Fall of France.

Listed by the Commonwealth War Graves Commission as having served as a Private with the number 4798018, their records show that Baden had been with the 1st/5th (Territorial) Battalion of the Sherwood Foresters. Another record, found in a different source, would later add even more detail to this by showing that he had served in their "A" Company. Further information contained in the war graves records also shows that his remains are interred at Sai Wan War Cemetery, which lies on the distant island of Hong Kong. Fortunately, the previously mentioned Derbyshire Times article provides us with the vital information that we need to see how this came to be the case. By informing us that he had been *"missing since the capitulation of Singapore"*, it therefore indicates that he had subsequently been held by the Japanese as a prisoner of war. Sadly, the date of his death confirms that he lost his life whilst he was still in their captivity.

After the evacuation of Dunkirk, Baden's battalion had remained in Britain until October 1941, when as a unit of 55th Brigade with the 18th Division, they had boarded a converted P&O Liner at Liverpool. Originally destined to take part in operations in North Africa that were aimed at lifting the siege of Tobruk, the Japanese invasion of Malaya, together with their almost simultaneous bombing of Pearl Harbour, brought about a rapid change to the plans for their deployment. As a result, they instead landed on the island of Singapore on 29th January 1942. Originally deployed to the North East of the island, they were regularly subjected to bombardment by the Japanese, who had already established air supremacy.

The first Japanese troops landed on the island on 8th February, and a constant struggle then ensued right up to the surrender on the 15th of that same month. To say that this defeat came as a shock to Britain and her Empire would be an understatement, and was an event that Churchill later described as *"The greatest disaster and capitulation in British history."*

Unfortunately, we have no details concerning Baden's time in captivity, but the atrocities committed by the Japanese in Singapore and elsewhere are as widely known as their reputation for the ill-treatment of prisoners of war. We also know that many of the men that were captured at Singapore were later put to work on the building of the infamous Burma Railway. Used as slave labourers to install its 258 miles of track, over 12,000 Allied prisoners of war are known to have died during the course of its construction, a figure equating to the loss of one life for every 38 yards. Whilst it is not known if Baden was involved with this work, it is only one of many known examples which demonstrate the systematic ill treatment that prisoners received at the hands of the Japanese. As a further example of this, a figure has been found which shows that over one third of the men captured with Baden's 18th Division did not survive their internment. However, we are told by the Commonwealth War Graves Commission that he had survived until February 1945, just six months short of liberation, and an additional source has been discovered which informs us that his death had resulted from Malaria.

MARPLES, R.

ROY MARPLES

An obituary for Roy Marples was printed in the Derbyshire Times on 16th March 1945 for which the informant, who is identified as having been a brother of the deceased, was named as Mr W. L. Marples of 145, Arkwright Town. Though brief, this source also provides us with several other useful details which include a confirmation that Roy had worked at Markham Colliery before the war.

This obituary also informs us that Roy had lost his parents at an early age, and had subsequently been adopted by a Mr and Mrs B. Thompson of 10, Arkwright Town. Using his age at death (supplied by the records of the Commonwealth War Graves Commission), we are able to find that Roy's birth was recorded in the Chesterfield district during the March ¼ of 1916. This source also provides us with the added detail that the maiden name of his mother had also been Thompson, and though no other supporting evidence has been found, this would strongly suggest that he had later been adopted by members of his mother's family.

After gathering further information from the Commonwealth War Graves Commission, which confirms that the Christian names of his parents were William and Jane, a record for the registration of their marriage is soon located showing that this had taken place in the Chesterfield district during the September ¼ of 1912. In addition to this, and by performing additional searches, we discover that the informant for the obituary had in fact been William, the couple's first child, and therefore Roy's eldest brother. More details found in the registration data tragically show that the death of both of Roy's parents was recorded in the September ¼ of 1920, when he would have been just 4 years old.

Unfortunately, the obituary that we have for Roy gives us very little information about his time in the army, though it does tell us that he had joined up in 1940. To obtain more details about his service we must therefore return to the records of the Commonwealth War Graves Commission. They show us that at the time of his death, he had been serving with the 4th Battalion of the Welch Regiment. A unit of the Territorial Army that could trace their origins back well beyond the formation of the Territorial Force in 1908, they had served in the United Kingdom and Northern Ireland until just after the Allied invasion of Normandy in June 1944. As part of the 160th Infantry Brigade with the 53rd (Welsh) Infantry Division, their first experience of overseas service, therefore, saw them straight away thrust into a baptism of fire amongst the hard-fought actions of the Normandy Campaign.

By early January 1945, the Allied advance had already made steady progress, and on the 9th of that month, Roy's battalion was located at a rest area near Liege. By this date no Germans remained beyond the West bank of the river Meuse, and the objective of the next phase of Allied operations was to drive them even further back to the banks of the Rhine. This, at last, took the 53rd (Welsh) Division over the border into Germany in the northern part of the Reichswald Forest, where they were to take part in Operation Veritable. This was the codename used for the northern part of a co-ordinated pincer movement which was to be mirrored by a similar offensive to the South, codenamed Operation Grenade, that was to be conducted by the US Ninth Army.

After a long hard struggle, the forest was eventually cleared of the enemy, and as the Northern pincer pushed even further forward, it liberated the towns of Kleve and Goch. Roy's battalion arrived on the outskirts of this latter place on 24th February and then, on 1st March, assisted the 7th Battalion of the Royal Welch Fusiliers in capturing the Weeze crossing on the river Niers. The envisaged link up of the Northern pincer with the American forces from the South happened on the 4th March at Berendonk near Geldern. By that date, Roy had possibly already been injured and evacuated back through the casualty clearing system, though his battalion did make a further attack at noon on the day that he died, and it is therefore just possible that he was injured in its early stages. This last action had the objective of capturing high ground near Alpon, which overlooked and therefore commanded a German crossing point on the Rhine at Wesel. Their enemy here were highly trained German paratroops who, operating from concealed positions in woodland, put up a stout resistance against Roy's battalion and exacted a heavy toll amongst them.

His obituary informs us that 30-year-old Roy, numbered as 3968046 and holding the rank of Corporal, died on 6th March as a result of wounds that he had received in action. His final resting place is in a small Commonwealth War Graves plot located within Turnhout Communal Cemetery, located within a Belgian municipality that lies approximately half way between Antwerp and Eindhoven.

ALVEY, J. K.

JOSEPH KIRBY ALVEY

The records of the Commonwealth War Graves Commission contain the details of only one casualty from the Second World War who had both the surname Alvey and "J" as a first initial. When examined more closely, they show him to have been Joseph Kirby Alvey, which is a perfect match for the inscription that we have on the memorial. Additionally, the personal details they hold for him establish a connection with our district (though not directly with Sutton-cum-Duckmanton) by describing him as being the *"Husband of Joyce Alvey, of Bolsover, Derbyshire."*

The final link in the chain, which makes this attribution certain by providing the vital connection to the parish, comes from a very small obituary that was published for him in the Derbyshire Times. In their edition dated for 27th April 1945 can be found an entry which simply reads:

"ALVEY – Guardsman Joseph Kirby Alvey (Grenadier Guards), aged 25 years, beloved son of Arthur and Nellie Alvey, Hill Top, Duckmanton, killed in action March 31st 1945."

Having discovered the names of his parents, we were then able to progress our investigation further using the registration data, and the first record to be found shows that Joseph's birth was documented in the Chesterfield district during the June ¼ of 1919. This also reveals that Kirby was the maiden name of his mother, and that this had, therefore, almost certainly been the inspiration for his unusual second Christian name. With that added detail it was soon established that the marriage of his parents had also taken place in the Chesterfield district, during the March ¼ of 1904.

With regard to his own marriage, another registration record made in the Chesterfield district, this time recorded during the December ¼ of 1941, informs us that his wife's maiden name had been Carter. The final record taken from this source, dating to the June ¼ of 1942, tells us of another happy event by showing us that the couple had gone on to have a son named Peter. It is incredibly poignant to discover that the personal inscription which appears on Joseph's headstone was written on behalf of this toddler. It is impossible not to be moved by it, despite it speaking of a loss that occurred almost eighty years ago.

"God bless my daddy, whom I shall only ever know in my dreams. Rest in peace my darling"

Returning to the records of the Commonwealth War Graves Commission for information about Joseph's service, we are told that numbered as 2625809, he had been a Guardsman with the 1st Battalion of the Grenadier Guards. As a unit of the 7th Guards Brigade within the 3rd Infantry Division, this battalion saw its first overseas service in France during late September 1939 as part of the British Expeditionary Force. Ultimately, this led to its evacuation from Dunkirk in 1940, and once back in Britain, it was assigned duties on home defence in response to the then impending threat of German invasion.

Further and more dramatic changes occurred in 1941, when the Guards regiments were converted into armoured units with the formation of the Guards Armoured Division. It would, however, be fair to say that this measure, designed to swell the number of tank units that could be deployed if the enemy crossed the English Channel, was frowned upon in some quarters. Almost certainly not well received by some of those who were already serving in these units, a certain amount of resistance had to be overcome. Whilst the Guards regiments as a whole were resolutely determined that they were not going to merely become a formation of the Royal Armoured Corps, the 1st Battalion of the Grenadiers were instead "motorised." This, however, was perhaps an acknowledgement that the sheer physical height of their men actually made it very difficult for them to fit inside the tanks of the day.

Issued with armoured cars, the men of Joseph's unit thus became the Motor Battalion of the 5th Guards Armoured Brigade, and were detailed to fulfil a special role in reconnaissance. A long period of training and familiarisation followed their conversion, and their return to overseas service was not made until late June 1944 when they landed in Normandy as part of VIII Corps. Their first major involvement in the hostilities swiftly followed with their taking part in Operation Goodwood, the codename given to the thrust inland that would allow the invasion force to break out of its beachhead. Proving that, despite being converted to armour, they were still able to uphold the best traditions of the Guards, this merely served as an introduction to their involvement in the hard slog needed to liberate France from the occupying German forces. It was, therefore, not long before they were in action again, this time to the East of Caen. After that, they were transferred to XXX Corps who would ultimately be responsible for the liberation of Brussels. Advancing further still, they took part in both Operation Market Garden during late September 1944 and Operation Veritable in February and March of the following year. This later advance being the one which saw them cross the border into Germany.

Joseph died on the 31st March 1945, and it is interesting to note, that, despite his obituary stating that he had been "killed in action", his final resting place is at Nijmegen in the Netherlands. Whilst the exact circumstances of his death are not known, it does perhaps seem more likely that he died of wounds after being evacuated through the casualty clearing system. The facts that his remains were interred at the Jonkerbos War Cemetery, which had been created by No3 Casualty Clearing Station, and that this is some distance away from where his unit were on that date would also seem to make this more likely. Joseph is also commemorated on the memorial that stands in the market place at Bolsover.

THE UNATTRIBUTABLE MEMORIAL INSCRIPTIONS FOR THE SECOND WORLD WAR

Unfortunately, there are two inscriptions for casualties of the Second World War that could not be attributed with any certainty. As we have already seen, a significant number of errors were found amongst the inscriptions concerning the casualties of the parish for the Great War, and unlike that earlier conflict, the engraved plate attached to the memorial for these later losses is the only source that we have for an original listing of their names. As a consequence of this, and because a number of errors were also found as our research progressed on the fallen of the Second World War, we have been unable to take any of the engraved names for this later conflict at face value. Both of the two unidentified casualties will, however, be discussed here in order to outline potential matches for them. In one way or another, all of the possibilities given for each of these inscriptions are equally compelling, and we have, therefore, been unable to select an identification for either that we can regard as more plausible than any of the other alternatives that we mention.

As with the casualties that we were unable to identify for the Great War, any information regarding either of these men would be gratefully received, and would allow any future editions of this work to be corrected and updated accordingly.

COOPER, R. T.
Initially, the identity of this man would seem easy to establish, as the files of the Commonwealth War Graves Commission contain records for only 3 men who had this combination of surname and initials. One of these is a Raymond Thomas Cooper of the Royal Australian Air Force. Whilst the family information that they provide for him does name his parents, there is no matching registration for any such wedding in the Chesterfield district

between 1880 and 1926, and no matching birth record for Raymond either.

The second possibility is a Robert Tysack Cooper of the Royal Navy. The family information that is available for him, however, shows a connection to Eastcote in Middlesex, and it is believed from other sources we have discovered that he was born in Norfolk. Again, no evidence has been found which connects this man to the parish of Sutton-cum-Duckmanton.

The third and final possibility is Richard Thomas Cooper of the Queen's Royal Regiment (West Surrey). The records of the Commonwealth War Graves Commission do not contain any information about his family, and whilst they do give his age at death, no matching entry for the registration of his birth was made in the Chesterfield district.

DANIEL, C. G.

Searching the records of the Commonwealth War Graves Commission returns only 2 results for anyone that could be described as "C. Daniel" that had been a casualty of the Second World War, and one of these could be ruled out of our investigations straight away because he was a Sepoy in the Indian Army. The second possibility, however, is a Clifford Daniel who lost his life whilst serving as a Navigator with the Royal Air Force Volunteer Reserve. Sadly, no evidence has been found to link him to the parish, and the data held on him by the Commonwealth War Graves Commission is not only completely devoid of any personal information about him, but does not even record his age at death. It should also be noted that their records merely refer to him as Clifford, giving no indication that he ever had a second Christian name.

There is, however, a third possibility for this man, a casualty who has the correct initials but a slightly different surname. This is Charles Gilchrist Daniels, who served as a 1st Class Stoker aboard the ill-fated H.M.S. Hood. It should, however, be noted that, according to the official website of the H.M.S. Hood Association, this man was born in Lambeth, and therefore seems to be just as unlikely a candidate as the others. Again, no evidence has been found to link this man to the parish.

SECOND WORLD WAR CASUALTIES ASSOCIATED WITH THE DISTRICT THAT ARE NOT NAMED ON THE MEMORIAL

As with the four additional casualties found for the Great War era, the following men are not named on the memorial despite evidence having been discovered which connects them to the local district. Again, there are many reasons why these names may not have been added originally, one of the most likely being that their families had moved out of the area leaving no one behind to remember them. It is also the case that they may have been excluded at the request of their next of kin, or because they were deemed not to qualify under the original terms that were drawn up for inclusion.

This is not intended to be a complete list of non-commemorations. These names and details merely surfaced during the course of our investigations into those who are named on the memorial, and there may be several others who have yet to be discovered. At this distance in time from the related events it would, in any case, be impossible to produce any list of non-commemorations that could be guaranteed to be complete.

Not falling under the terms of reference for the original project, these details are, however, given here in respectful acknowledgement of their sacrifice.

982392, Corporal Joseph Brown, Royal Air Force Volunteer Reserve who fell 5th July 1941. Linked by information held by the Commonwealth War Graves Commission which states that he was the *"Son of Joseph and Rose Brown; husband of Sybil E. Brown, of Duckmanton, Derbyshire."*

C/NX 1480, Canteen Manager George Thomas Cockett, Royal Naval Canteen Service who fell 8th November 1942. Linked by information held by the Commonwealth War Graves Commission which states that he was the *"Son of George Henry and Lily Cockett; husband of Gladys Freda Cockett, of Duckmanton, Derbyshire."*

SOURCES

PRIMARY

Army Pension Records
Army Service Records
Battalion War Diaries
Derbyshire Parish Records
England census 1891
England census 1901
England census 1911
Medal Index Cards
Medal Rolls for the 1914 Star
Medal Rolls for the 1914-15 Star
Medal Rolls for the British War and Victory Medals
Ministry of Pensions – Hospital and CCS Locations
Registers of Soldiers Effects
Silver War Badge Rolls
Sundry other newspapers accessed via the British Newspaper
    Archive
The 1939 Register
The Derbyshire Courier 1914-20
The Derbyshire Times and Chesterfield Herald 1914-45

SECONDARY

"9th Service Battalion The Sherwood Foresters" – Morse
"10th (S) Battalion The Sherwood Foresters" – Hoyte
"A History of the 10th Battalion The Notts & Derbys" – Osborne
"First in Last Out" – Housley
"Grenadier Guards in The War of 1939-1945" – Nicholson
"Officers Died in The Great War" – transcription on CD-ROM
"Soldiers Died in The Great War" – transcription on CD-ROM
"The 1st and 2nd Battalions The Sherwood Foresters in The Great
    War" – Wylly
"The British Reconnaissance Corps in World War II" – Doherty
    & Chapman
"The First Day on the Somme" – Middlebrook
"The Grenadier Guards in The Great War of 1914-19" –
    Ponsonby

"The History of the Prince of Wales' s Own Civil Service
    Rifles" – Various
"The Register of Chesterfield and District Great War
    Memorials" (Authors own unpublished work)
"The Somme: The Day by Day Account" - McCarthy
"Tommy" - Holmes

WEBSITES

4thBattalionTF.pdf
Aircrewremembered.com
Britain at war.org
Commonwealth War Graves Commission
FreeBmd records of births, marriages and deaths
Google Maps
International Bomber Command Centre
National Archives of Australia (website)
Naval-History.net (website)
Royalwelsh.org.uk/downloads/E05-03-WelchR-WW2-
The Great War Forum
The Long Long Trail
The National Archives (TNA)
The official website of the H.M.S. Hood Association
The official website of the Royal Leicestershire Regiment.
Wikipedia
Ww2db.com
WW2talk.com
www.89fss.com/affiliated/22indcoy
www.paradata.org.uk

IMAGES

All portraits are drawn from The Derbyshire Courier or
Derbyshire Times except for those of W. E. Ind which was drawn
from "The History of the Prince of Wales' s Own Civil Service
Rifles" and that of A. W. Bowles which came from a private
source. Without exception, all images used have been subjected to
an intensive process of restoration and enhancement by the
author.
All cap badge illustrations are the author's own photographs.
Memorial cover picture – author's own photograph.
Memorial Scroll back cover illustration – author's own image.
Thiepval Memorial picture – author's own image.

BIOGRAPHIES INDEX

NOTES